Answer the Question:
Get the Job!

Answer the Question: Get the Job!

101 Interview Questions and How to Answer Them

by Iain Maitland

CENTURY
BUSINESS

First published in the UK 1993
by Century Business

An imprint of Random House UK Ltd
20 Vauxhall Bridge Road, London SW1V 2SA

Random House Australia (Pty) Ltd
20 Alfred Street, Milsons Point
Sydney, NSW 2061, Australia

Random House New Zealand Ltd
18 Poland Road, Glenfield,
Aukland 10, New Zealand

Random House South Africa (Pty) Ltd
PO Box 337, Bergvlei, South Africa

Typeset by SX Composing, Rayleigh, Essex
Printed and bound in Great Britain by
Mackays of Chatham PLC, Chatham, Kent

A catalogue record for this book is available from the British Library

ISBN 0-7126-5763-0

To Tracey, Michael and Sophie

CONTENTS

PREFACE

This book is written for you – the prospective interviewee who is about to face a job or employment interview, perhaps for the first time. Taking you step by step through your interview, it looks closely at one hundred and one of the most popular questions. You are told when and why they are asked, how they may be phrased and how you should reply. Model answers are given for each and every one of them, to show you how to be a winner.

'Preparing for Your Interview' tells you how to research the organisation, get to know yourself better, investigate the interview and be a successful interviewee. Read the chapter carefully, for without this background knowledge and work you have absolutely no chance of success. 'The Opening Moments' explains how to tackle the early stages of your interview – arriving at the organisation, approaching the interview room, listening to the interviewer's comments and answering preliminary questions. Make sure you get off to a good start.

'Education, Qualifications and Training' details the questions that your interviewer may raise when focusing on your education, examining your qualifications and talking about training, and provides you with the best responses. 'Employment Issues' lists the many questions that will be fired at you when discussing your previous employment. The interviewer will also question you about how you view this vacancy and contemplate your future employment. You must be ready with winning replies.

'Personality Matters' sets out the questions which may be asked when your interviewer wishes to probe your personality and look at your leisure activities. Some questions might even go so far as to invade your privacy – and you may not want to answer those ones. 'Miscellaneous Topics' notes the questions that can crop up when the interviewer wants to put you to the test. It also incorporates offbeat and fact-checking questions, and tells you how to handle them effectively.

'The Closing Stages' examines dealing with the final questions that round off the interview, leaving the interview room and what you should do when you are going home, to be successful. 'Action Checklists', '101 Questions: A Checklist', 'Further Reading' and 'Useful Addresses' complete the book – and help to make it a valuable, hands-on guide to interviewing success, whether you are a school or college leaver or a management executive seeking to climb the career ladder.

Iain Maitland

ACKNOWLEDGEMENTS

Thanks are due to those organisations which provided me with information regarding recruitment and work interviews, particularly Barclays Bank plc, the Boots Company plc, the Halifax Building Society, Imperial Chemical Industries plc, the Institute of Management, the Metropolitan Police, Selfridges and Wimpy International. Special thanks to the interviewers and interviewees – too numerous to mention individually – who discussed their selection, job hunting and employment experiences with me. Thank you, one and all.

1 PREPARING FOR YOUR INTERVIEW

Researching the Organisation
Knowing Yourself
Investigating the Interview
Being a Successful Interviewee

PREPARING FOR YOUR INTERVIEW

Whatever type of interview you are about to attend – perhaps for your first job or an in-house transfer or promotion – you must prepare for it in a comprehensive and thorough manner. Detailed preparation is the key to your success. You have to re-search the organisation, know yourself well, investigate the interview and understand the basic do's and don'ts of being a successful interviewee. Only when you have completed this essential background work will you be ready and able to walk confidently into the interview room, impress the interviewer and leave as a winner.

RESEARCHING THE ORGANISATION

If you have applied for a job, been invited to an interview and accepted that invitation, you will inevitably have conducted some research to make sure the organisation and work are suited to you, and vice versa. Even so, you ought to refresh and pos-sibly develop your knowledge before the interview to convince yourself and subsequently the interviewer that you really are well matched. Should you not have carried out any research to date – perhaps because you have been automatically asked along for an interview as you were next in line when the vacancy arose – you now need to find out all you can about:

– The Organisation
– The Job
– The Ideal Employee

3

THE ORGANISATION
Discover everything there is to know about the organisation. For example, who owns it? How is it structured? Who are the key personnel? How many workers are employed? What do the various departments and employees do? Where is it based? How many other outlets exist? Where are these located? How are they organised and run? Look into its activities, too. As examples, what exactly does it do? What products does it sell? What services does it offer? What are their strengths and weaknesses? What is its annual turnover? Is this increasing, or decreasing? What are its goals? What is its reputation like?

Contemplate its marketplace. What market does the organisation operate in? Is this expanding, static or contracting? What is its market share? Is this improving, or not? Find out about its customers as well. For example, who are they? What do they do? Where do they live and work? What do they want from the organisation? Think about its rivals. What are their main features? What are their particular pluses and minuses? How well do these competitors seem to be doing in the market? All in all, how is the marketplace changing and developing over time?

Most of these questions can be answered easily, by simple research. Read through the job advertisement and that letter inviting you to the interview. They should contain snippets of useful information, typically about the owners, the outlets, their locations and so forth. If you have not already perused the organisation's literature – which you ought to have done prior to applying for the post – obtain as much as possible now. Study annual reports, sales brochures, catalogues and price lists to widen your understanding in all areas. Visit the organisation if you can, taking a look around and chatting to staff to fill in any gaps in your knowledge. Examine goods, handling and using them to learn about their good and bad points.

Further data about the organisation and the marketplace may be built up by talking to relatives, friends, business acquaintances, customers and rival concerns. Reference books – *The Directory of British Associations, The Times Top 1000, Key British*

4

Enterprises and the like – can be found in libraries, and contain a wealth of detailed information. Local, national and international surveys, reports and statistics produced by chambers of commerce, local councils, the Government and so on may be stocked there as well. Approach appropriate British trade associations for advice and read local, national and trade newspapers, magazines and journals as regularly as possible. Do anything and everything you can think of to find out all you can.

THE JOB

Similarly, you want to be fully familiar with the job that you have applied for within the organisation. Again, numerous questions need to be asked, and answered. What is the job title? What is the purpose of the job? Who and what will the job holder be responsible for? Who will he or she be responsible to? What tasks will the job holder have to do? How much will he be paid? What are the terms and conditions of the job? How exactly does the job fit into the organisation? How does it relate to other departments and employees? What are the working conditions like? How is the job going to develop?

It should be relatively straightforward for you to respond instantly to many or even all of these various queries. You probably will have gathered together a substantial amount of information from the recruitment advertisement, any preliminary telephone conversations with employees of the organisation and the application form and its accompanying material such as an information sheet. More details could have been added from the organisation's other literature, by chatting to staff if you visited the premises, through talking to contacts including those people who do similar work in comparable concerns and by reading relevant newspapers, magazines, journals and books.

Of prime importance, always ask the organisation to send you a job description. This one- or two-page statement details the job title along with its key purpose, main responsibilities and tasks and the job titles of superiors and subordinates. It tells you exactly how the organisation views the job. Of equal significance, try to talk to the vacating job holder if you can. He or she may complete your understanding of the job by informing you precisely how this list of duties translates into practice on a day-to-day basis.

THE IDEAL EMPLOYEE

You ought to be aware of the type of person that the organisation is seeking to recruit for the post. You may wish to discover the ideal physical make-up of the successful candidate. For example, should he or she be a particular sex, age, race, height or weight? What about his or her appearance? Is that important? How about his or her speech? Is this significant? What about his or her health? Are good eyesight and hearing necessary to do the job properly? Find out about the attainments that the winning candidate is expected to have. As examples, how well educated must he or she be? What qualifications should he or she possess? What training courses ought to have been attended? Is previous work experience relevant? If so, what type of experience is preferred?

Consider the intelligence of the chosen candidate. Should he or she be able to learn quickly? Is a good memory needed for this job? Is common sense important? Contemplate any specific aptitudes that the employee ought to possess. Should he or she require a head for figures, a flair for writing or a talent for artistic work? Think about any interests that he or she might have. Are sporting pursuits relevant to this job? Would literary interests be of benefit? Are artistic hobbies likely to enable the job holder to be more successful at his or her work?

Not surprisingly, the organisation will attach key significance to the employee's disposition. Does he or she need to be able to communicate well? Are honesty and reliability relevant qualities? Must he or she be motivated and willing to work hard? Should he or she be friendly? Is maturity important? Must he or she be a team person? Should he or she be capable of working alone, using his or her initiative? The ideal employee's circumstances may be of some importance, too. Must he or she have a car? Is a clean driving licence necessary? Does he or she need to possess a telephone?

You ought to find it relatively simple to answer most of these numerous questions. The job advertisement will have stated the main qualities required, perhaps specifying an age range, the minimum number and type of qualifications needed, the importance of previous work experience in this trade or industry, and so on. Talking to existing employees in the organisation, business acquaintances in similar jobs and – most appropriate of all – the outgoing job holder will allow you to expand your understanding of the ideal employee and his or her various qualities.

Of crucial assistance, request an employee specification from the organisation. Also known as a job, person or personnel specification, this is a one- or two-sided statement that is drawn up alongside the job description. It details the type of person needed with the assorted skills, knowledge and experiences grouped into essential and desirable requirements – he or she *must* have a clean and tidy appearance, and so on; he or she *should* have previous office experience, and so forth. If such a specification is not available, work it out for yourself. Take each of the duties listed in the job description and calculate the attributes needed to do them properly.

KNOWING YOURSELF

Having accumulated all of this valuable knowledge about the organisation, job and type of employee required, you need to step back and look at yourself. You have to be sure that the organisation really is right for you, and vice versa. It is important to feel certain that you can do the job. You must be convinced that you are the ideal person on this occasion, *and* that the organisation will think so, too. Otherwise, there is little point in

RESEARCHING THE ORGANISATION: AN ACTION CHECKLIST

Discover all you can about the organisation, job and ideal employee. Take a large sheet of paper and jot down everything you uncover beneath these headings.

The Organisation	The Job	The Ideal Employee

going on any further. You will simply be wasting the interviewer's time, and your own. Typically, you might look in turn at:

– Your Personality
– Your Strengths
– Your Weaknesses

YOUR PERSONALITY

Start off by considering yourself as a person, being as brutally honest as anyone can be when assessing themselves. Try to compose a list of ten or so words and phrases which provide a comprehensive description of your personality. As an example, you may begin by putting down that you are 'a natural leader' who 'likes to take charge of a team' and 'carry out tasks in my own way'. You are 'ambitious' and 'hardworking', and 'equally demanding of others'. You 'do not suffer fools gladly, especially those who let the team down', and so on. See yourself as other people do, attempting to sketch out both good *and* bad aspects of your personality.

Then imagine yourself being employed by this organisation to decide if you are well matched. Go through each of your key words and phrases, comparing and contrasting them carefully with what you have learned about the firm. A small business with few outlets may not be able to satisfy your ambitions, whereas a larger concern might do. Contemplate your various pluses and minuses alongside the job. Working alone may not be ideal for a natural leader who is more suited to teamwork. Think about that ideal employee, and whether your qualities tie up with the requirements listed on the employee specification. A hard worker may be sought – but perhaps not one who is equally demanding of others.

As a double check, it is a sensible idea to ask a trusted friend or close relative to write down ten words and phrases which describe you. Most people view themselves in a favourable light and tend to note more of their positive rather than negative features. Even minuses are transformed into pluses. You may have stated that you 'have an eye for detail'. Your friend could claim that you are 'a nitpicker'. You might say you are 'laid back'. Your relative may describe you as 'a lazy so-and-so'. Compare his or her (more realistic) list alongside the organisation, job and ideal employee. Does this person – perhaps the 'real' you – sound suitable in the circumstances?

YOUR STRENGTHS

Next, review the skills, knowledge and experience that you have built up over the years, through your education, employment and leisure interests. Jot down ten key achievements that you are particularly proud of. You may note that you were 'a prefect at school' and obtained 'eight GCSEs, all A and B grades'. You 'worked in an old people's home in the holidays' and were 'offered full-time employment there on leaving school'. In your 'first job as an office junior', you were 'promoted within the year', and 'received a substantial pay rise'. In the evenings, you 'went to college' and 'learned to use computers'. You are 'captain of the local hockey team', and so forth.

Work out how relevant these achievements are to the organisation. Knowing about computers may be helpful in a computerised firm but is far less relevant in a business which maintains its books and records on a manually operated basis. Similarly, compare your skills, knowledge and experience with the job you are applying for. Caring for elderly ladies and gentlemen may be a useful experience if the job involves dealing with customers, especially older ones. It is less significant if you will be working on a production line in a factory. Mull over what you have to offer with what is expected of the ideal employee. A former prefect and a current team captain probably has leadership skills which may be considered essential for a department head, but unnecessary for someone working further down the line.

Take another look at the application form that you completed

11

or the curriculum vitae which you submitted to the organisation. This must have been impressive enough for the interviewer to have invited you in for an interview. Knowing what you now know about the organisation, job and person required, try to spot any other strengths that you have not included on your list. Perhaps you overlooked your driving licence because it took you four attempts to pass your test. Nevertheless, the firm may see this licence as a plus, as it makes you a more mobile employee. Possibly, you did not note down that you own a fax machine because it did not occur to you that the organisation might regard this as a strength, as it likes some of its employees to work from home.

YOUR WEAKNESSES
Of course, everyone has had their share of setbacks and failures and it is wise to face up to them. Thinking over your education, employment and leisure interests again, sketch out up to ten weaknesses that you are unhappy about. You might write down that you were 'suspended from school for two weeks for repeatedly breaking the rules' concerning your appearance. You achieved 'two A levels with E grades, and only after resits'. You were 'dismissed from a job because I was unable to do the work properly'. You have 'had the same job for six years without promotion, despite several in-house applications being made'.

Then relate these weaknesses to the organisation that you wish to join. Being suspended from school may indicate that you will have problems complying with the strict rules and regulations of some businesses. Mull over the relevance of your shortcomings in relation to the work you are expected to do. Being dismissed from a job which was similar to this one might not be a good sign. Consider the person required by the organisation to actually do the job. Having held the same post for some time could suggest you are not the 'dynamic go-getter' that this company wishes to recruit, and so forth.

Once more, check through that application form or curriculum vitae, just to see if you can spot any other weaknesses that have not been incorporated in your notes. Perhaps your current salary is at the uppermost limit of the range that is offered by the organisation, which could count against you since the interviewer may be inclined towards taking on another, less expensive person. Possibly, you are at the lower or higher end of the age range required, and may feel that your interviewer would prefer someone in the middle who is neither 'too green' nor 'over the hill'.

Hopefully, your rigorous self-analysis will help you to conclude whether you are right for this job – and do remember that the interviewer must think you are, otherwise he or she would not have asked you along for an interview. As important, it allows you really to get to know yourself well. It helps you to focus upon your strengths which you will then be ready to refer to in your answers at the interview. It also enables you to identify your weaknesses which you need to contemplate and will probably have to discuss at your interview to prove to the interviewer that you are the best person for the job, despite your flaws.

INVESTIGATING THE INTERVIEW

Now that you are wholly familiar with the organisation, the job and the type of employee required, *and* are convinced that you are the right person in this instance, you should give your full attention to the interview itself. You need to mull over this important occasion which may well prove to be a turning point in your career, building up your knowledge and understanding so that you have a better idea of what to expect of:

– The Interview
– The Interviewer
– The Questions

13

KNOWING YOURSELF: AN ACTION CHECKLIST

Take a long, hard look at yourself as part of your research. Completing a checklist like this one may help you to get to know yourself better – especially if a close friend or relative fills it in for you!

Your Personality	Your Strengths	Your Weaknesses
1.	1.	1.
2.	2.	2.
3.	3.	3.
4.	4.	4.

5.

6.

7.

8.

9.

10.

5.

6.

7.

8.

9.

10.

5.

6.

7.

8.

9.

10.

THE INTERVIEW
Almost certainly, you are about to attend a selection interview for a job. You may be pursuing a post in a firm which you have approached for the first time, or you might be chasing transfer or promotion to another position within your own organisation. If successful, you will subsequently face various employment interviews – 'induction' to ease you into the job, 'appraisal' to see how you are progressing, 'discipline', 'grievance' and 'counselling' if problems occur and 'exit' interviews to discover why you are leaving. Whether a selection, appraisal or even an exit interview, there are many characteristics which are common to all, and which can be readily identified and thought about by you beforehand.

Selection, induction, appraisal interviews and the rest can be regrouped into two categories – 'one-to-one' and 'panel' interviews. As the name suggests, one-to-one – or 'individual' – interviews are those in which one interviewer faces you, the interviewee. This is the most common type of interview. You will probably meet a personnel manager or the head of the department that you will work in if you are successful. One-to-ones are popular with both interviewers and interviewees – it is easy to arrange an agreeable date, time and place as only two people are involved, the interviewer can control and lead the conversation as he or she wishes, and you will find it relatively informal, and as relaxing as any interview can be. As a consequence, it should be possible for both of you to establish a relationship, build a rapport and find out all about each other.

However, there is a major drawback relating to one-to-one interviews so far as you are concerned. One person – that man or woman on the other side of the desk – makes (or strongly influences) the decisions about whether you are suitable or unsuitable for the position. If he or she is untrained, inexperienced, has sexist or racist attitudes or whatever, you could be rejected, despite your many qualities and suitability for this particular job. No matter what you do or say, you might lose out through no fault of your own. Although this happens rarely, it is a persistent worry.

Panel interviews – or 'boards' as they are also known – comprise several interviewers facing you. Perhaps you will sit opposite three to six interviewers, including a personnel manager, department heads who come into contact with the job, a specialist in the field and trainee interviewers sitting in to gain experience. In their favour, board interviews do enable interviewers to share the workload and responsibilities between them and to impress the importance of the occasion on you. They appear impressive and businesslike. Most significant of all, increasing the number of interviewers boosts your chances of a fair and equal hearing, since it is less likely that every interviewer will be untrained, inexperienced and so on.

Nevertheless, panel interviews do have numerous disadvantages. It is hard to gather everyone together at a mutually acceptable time and place, and interviewers have been known to work individually instead of as a team, thus dragging you into their in-house rivalries and petty squabbles. Facing a row of interviewers – perhaps stern-faced and daunting – can be enormously stressful, making you feel tense and far less able to perform to the best of your abilities. It may be very difficult to create the easy-going and open atmosphere that is so necessary for a full and frank exchange of views.

Whether a one-to-one or panel interview, it should be conducted in a peaceful and undisturbed atmosphere where questions can be asked and answered without distracting noises being heard or interruptions taking place. Ideally, the interview will be held in a quiet office, with perhaps a desk and chairs facing each other, or easy chairs in which the interviewer(s) and you can sit, relax and discuss matters. The room should be free of distractions such as the sun shining in your face, so that you can both (or all) concentrate on the task ahead. Of course, interviews can be carried out almost anywhere – from a classroom to a pub – but should always be detached from the hurly-burly of business or social life.

Whatever type of interview is held – selection, counselling or exit – it will have a broadly comparable beginning, middle and end to other types. The beginning will consist of the initial meeting between the interviewer(s) and you, followed by introductions, small talk and gentle questions to ease both parties into the interview. The middle will comprise the cut and thrust of questions and answers as the reasons behind the interview are probed, explained and discussed in some detail. The ending will consist of a rounding up of the discussions, an agreement on what was said and what will happen next, plus goodbyes.

Your interview could last for almost any length of time, from perhaps ten minutes to one and a half hours, or even more. Obviously, it all depends upon what is to be covered, and individual circumstances. A selection interview with a young person with little behind him to talk about except his education may last for twenty minutes or so, whereas a corresponding interview with a manager with thirty years' employment behind her could run on for well over an hour. Similarly, a counselling interview concerning a minor matter might last for just ten minutes, an exit interview much longer. As a very rough-and-ready rule of thumb, thirty minutes is probably the average duration for an interview.

THE INTERVIEWER

Not surprisingly, all interviewers are different – experienced and inexperienced, good and bad, and so on. You are most likely to face just one interviewer and hopefully he or she will be trained and able enough to conduct the interview properly, having attended courses, read books and sat in on other interviews before being left in charge. He or she will be well prepared. The interview will start on time. Your details will be laid out across the desk. The interviewer will have worked out a loose and flexible plan, knowing what topics need to be covered, and which questions should be asked and answered. This plan is adhered to, with your conversation being kept to the point, and notes being taken about comments made.

He or she will be fair and open-minded, attempting to establish rapport by making small talk. The interviewer will allow you to answer and explain, and will listen carefully to what is said. A decision will not be made until all of the interviews have been completed, so that each and every interviewee is given an equal opportunity to prove his suitability or unsuitability. He or she conducts the interview in a quiet place in order that both parties can concentrate on your discussions, and lets it run long enough to cover all the key points, but not so long that the same topics are covered over and again.

Of course, you may face a poor interviewer who is untrained and is carrying out the interview simply because he or she is the head of the department. The interviewer could be ill-prepared, with interviews running late, details mislaid and topics and questions tackled in a haphazard fashion. Even worse, he or she might make an instant decision about you and then spend the remainder of the interview trying to substantiate this opinion. The interviewer may talk endlessly about irrelevant subjects, interrupt as and when he or she feels like doing so, and may not listen to what you say. The interview might be held in a noisy place, and be cut short when he or she has had enough. Fortunately such interviewers are few and far between but you may come up against one. Do not worry though – all of this excellent preparation and your interview skills will see you through, no matter what.

THE QUESTIONS

Various types of question will arise during your interview, and these are sometimes called 'open', 'closed', 'limited', 'leading', 'hypothetical' and 'multiple' questions. Open questions begin with words such as 'Why', 'How' and 'What', as in 'Why did you go to that school?', 'How well do you expect to do in your exams?' and 'What training have you had?' They are asked often, and should be seen as marvellous opportunities to explain and discuss thoughts and opinions. Hopefully, your interviewer will raise these questions frequently so that you can put across your knowledge about the organisation and job, talk through your qualities and show how well suited you are to the post.

Closed questions are the opposite of open ones, allowing only a 'Yes' or 'No' response, as in reply to 'Did you benefit from that training?' and 'Did you like that job?' Used to check facts and to keep nervous interviewees talking, it is sensible to treat them as open questions, replying along the lines of 'Yes, I benefited from that training in several ways. First of all . . .' or 'Yes, I did like the job because . . .' Limited questions start with words such as 'Who', 'When', 'Where' and 'Which', as in 'Who was your boss?' and 'Which newspaper do you read?' Again, tackle them as open questions, developing your answers to promote your strengths: 'George Seabrook . . . we worked very well to–gether . . .', and so on.

Leading questions are those which signpost the answer that should be given, as with 'Do you have initiative?', 'Can you work to a deadline?' and 'Are you willing to move about?' The answers are obvious. Only foolish interviewers phrase questions in this way since you will simply give the 'right' response which will tell the interviewer nothing new at all. Wiser interviewers rephrase them as open questions such as 'How do you show initiative?', 'What do you do when faced with deadlines?' and 'How do you feel about relocating?' so that you have to talk in more detail. If asked a leading question, give the 'correct' answer but then add to it to show your strengths, 'Yes, I have initiative. As an example of this, at my last job I had to . . .'

Hypothetical questions tend to crop up now and again in interviews and involve the interviewer asking you what you would do in a given situation: 'How would you handle this task?' and 'What would you do if the following event took place?' are examples. You should be able to calculate what the ideal employee would do, and give the right answer in the circumstances: 'I'd approach the task in a calm and logical manner. I'd assess the situation, look at the options available and would then . . .' Multiple questions are those where several questions run into one: 'What do you do in the evenings and at weekends? I mean do you have any hobbies or belong to any clubs or societies?' These are easy to answer. Separate them, and then respond, one at a time.

BEING A SUCCESSFUL INTERVIEWEE

No matter what type of interview you are going to attend, and regardless of the interviewer you will meet and the questions he or she will ask, you should be able to walk into that interview knowing how to be a winning interviewee. Whatever your individual situation, there are numerous do's and don'ts that you can follow which are applicable in all instances, whether you are facing a selection or promotion interview, an experienced or inexperienced interviewer, open or closed questions, and so on. Thus, you need to be familiar with:

- The Do's of Interviewing Success
- The Don'ts of Interviewing Success

THE DO'S OF INTERVIEWING SUCCESS

Be well prepared for your interview. It is tedious and time-consuming to research the organisation, think about yourself and learn about interviews, but it really is worthwhile. With all of this background knowledge, you can enter the room knowing that you and the job are right for each other. You will be able to converse freely about the organisation, the job and the ideal employee and why you are the best person for the post. You will be aware of what to expect from the interview and your interviewer and the types of question you will be asked. Without all of this preliminary work, you would know very little, inevitably coming out as a failure – and deservedly so.

Do make sure that you know precisely when *and* where your interview is being held, checking the letter inviting you to the interview and any accompanying map, or telephoning the organisation to confirm the time and place if necessary. Turning up late so that the interviewer's schedule is thrown into confusion or not arriving at all and then asking for a rearranged date will mark you down as a loser. Carry out a trial run the day before the interview is due to be held so that you are conscious of how long it takes you to travel there. Allow an extra thirty

INVESTIGATING THE INTERVIEW: AN ACTION CHECKLIST

Find out as much as possible about interviews before attending yours. To refresh your memory, write down what you learned on a piece of paper, using these headings.

The Interview	The Interviewer	The Questions

minutes or so on the day itself, just in case the bus is delayed or your car breaks down.

Pay attention to your appearance, which is likely to be considered important by almost all employers, especially if the job involves face-to-face contact with customers. Dress in an appropriate manner for the particular position, mindful that an executive in an advertising agency may be eccentric with his hair tied up in a ponytail and wearing a floral shirt, whereas a trainee bank clerk cannot be. Avoid fashionable and loud clothes, and extravagant jewellery. If in doubt, a sober suit, white shirt or blouse, tie, dark socks or tights and black shoes could be regarded as the interviewee's uniform. It may be boring, but it is safe, and acceptable to everyone.

Personal hygiene is closely associated with your appearance. Clearly, there is little or no point in wearing the right clothes for the occasion if you have bad breath and body odour, and the clothes are filthy and stained. No one wants to employ a dirty worker who will alienate his or her colleagues and customers. Wash your hair, have a bath or shower, clean those teeth, use a deodorant, scrub your nails and put on washed and ironed clothes, and polished shoes. Steer away from smoking, drinking alcohol and eating immediately before the interview, to help to maintain cleanliness.

Difficult though it may be to acheive, especially if you are a first-time interviewee, do attempt to be as relaxed as you can during the interview. Tense, hunched up and forcing out your answers in a strangulated stutter will create a very poor impression indeed. Take deep breaths and count from one to ten beforehand, which may loosen you up. In the interview room, lean slightly forward with your hands held in your lap and your legs tucked in under your chair. Keep still, without shifting in your seat, jiggling with a pen or making sudden movements. Appear as though you are in control.

Look at the interviewer as he or she speaks, *and* as you reply. If there are several interviewers, watch the person talking and look at each of them as you answer. Avoiding eye contact, staring at your feet or gazing out of the window makes you seem

24

shifty and disinterested. Appear interested throughout, by nodding, smiling and nudging the conversation along with an 'mmm', 'yes', 'go on' and so forth. Listen to what is being said, instead of mulling over your last response or what you will say in answer to the next question. Mishearing 'What newspaper do you read?' as '. . . Do you read?' will generate an inappropriate reply which will confuse the interviewer, and not impress him or her at all.

Try to answer each and every question that is put to you. Hear the question, considering why it has been asked and what the interviewer wants to find out. Think over what you have discovered during your research and phrase your reply so that you show your strengths and substantiate them, perhaps by giving examples. Typically, your interviewer may ask you to describe your last job and you decide that this is to see if you have the necessary previous experience to do this work. You contemplate the two posts and discuss their similarities, backing up your comments with descriptions of various specialised tasks so that it is obvious that you did them.

Tell the truth at all times. Of course, you will be selective in what you say, promoting your positive rather than your negative features as far as you can, but you should avoid exaggerating or being dishonest. Experienced interviewers may be able to spot that you do not know what you are talking about and could recognise contradictions. Certificates may need to be produced and teachers and former employers will be approached for references, perhaps via off-the-record telephone conversations. You run the risk of being found out either now or later on after you have started work, when you may be dismissed without references. If you feel that you can succeed only by lying, then this suggests you are ill-suited to the position – so look for another job.

Make certain that you speak clearly and steadily at your interview, so you are heard *and* understood. Avoid gabbling, slurring your speech and talking into your lap, which will obscure what you are saying. Try not to speak too slowly though, as the interviewer may believe you are either slow-witted or patronising him or her. Steer away from confusing slang, offensive bad language and irritating words and phrases such as 'actually' and 'you know'. Use your natural voice rather than a false one which is hard to sustain, and attempt to sound keen and enthusiastic about whatever you say. If you are not, you cannot expect the interviewer to be.

Stay calm, no matter what happens. If the telephone rings or someone enters the room, pause, remember what you were talking about and be ready to continue when your interviewer indicates you should do. If you cannot answer a question, admit it rather than struggling on helplessly or spouting nonsense. Add that you will discover the answer or ask him or her to tell you, whichever seems most appropriate. If your mind goes blank, say so and suggest that you move on, coming back to the topic or question in a moment or two. If your interviewer becomes argumentative to test you under pressure, remain reasonable as you reply. Staying cool shows you are confident and in control of the situation – and that you are a winner.

THE DON'TS OF INTERVIEWING SUCCESS

It is important that you do not become overfamiliar with your interviewer, however well you seem to be getting on. Naturally, you will seek to build up a friendly, professional relationship by maintaining a slight physical distance, referring to him or her as 'Mr Smith' or 'Mrs Thompson' and saying 'please' and 'thank you' when relevant. Do not go to extremes though. Shifting your chair next to his or hers, calling him or her 'Peter' or 'Sarah' and repeating 'please' and 'thank you' at the end of each sentence will lose you the job. Remember that the interviewer is not your friend but a would-be employer who wishes to maintain a businesslike association with you, and no more. Keep it like that.

Try not to become impatient at any time during the course of the interview, and certainly never show it if you do. Let the interviewer finish the question before you reply, even if you are sure that you know what he or she is about to say. You will appear rude and arrogant if you butt in mid-sentence, and should you misjudge what he or she was going to ask, will make yourself look very foolish, too. Equally important, do not be in a hurry to break up silences, as momentary lulls are normal in every conversation. Almost inevitably, you will interrupt the interviewer's thoughts or phrasing of the next question.

As a golden rule, avoid talking too much when you respond to questions. Listen to the question, work out precisely what you have to say to make your point, express yourself in a clear and concise manner, and shut up. Going on and on and on, repeating the same facts over and over again in different ways and from alternative angles will simply mark you out as a dithering windbag. Also, you will inevitably have been allocated a set time for your interview, perhaps thirty minutes. Ensure that all topics and questions are covered by being thorough *and* efficient from start to finish.

Likewise, make certain that anything you say is absolutely relevant. An initial query about your journey should not be seen as an opportunity for you to give a blow-by-blow account of your adventures since awaking this morning. A question concerning your academic career must not be regarded as your chance to lecture the interviewer on the inadequacies of the education system as you see them. Recognise why each question is put to you, refer to your strengths, back them up with examples as and where possible. Tell the interviewer what he or she wishes to hear, and nothing else.

Never become involved in a heated exchange with your interviewer even if you disagree with or are upset by what he or she says. Be conscious that some interviewers will deliberately try to provoke you, perhaps by making outrageous statements or expressing disbelief at your answers. Whether staged or genuine, stand up for yourself and your opinions, working through or restating your comments in a cool and reasoned manner. Hold your ground without turning aggressive or abusive. Lose your temper – lose the job.

27

BEING A SUCCESSFUL INTERVIEWEE: AN ACTION CHECKLIST

Probably the best advice to give a would-be interviewee is this:
do learn these do's and don'ts and do not forget them!

* Do prepare well for your interview

* Do not become overfamiliar with the interviewer

* Do arrive on time

* Do not become impatient at any time

* Do take care of your appearance

* Do not talk too much

* Do pay attention to personal hygiene

* Do not be irrelevant

* Do try to relax during the interview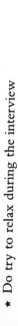

* Do look at and listen to your interviewer

* Do answer the questions put to you

* Do be truthful at all times

* Do speak clearly as you reply

* Do stay calm

* Do not be argumentative

* Do not criticise anyone

* Do not show off

* Do not worry – you are a winner!

Do not criticise anyone at your interview, as critical comments can make you appear petty and immature. It is very tempting to blame everyone else for your weaknesses as and when these arise during your conversation with the interviewer. Typically, teachers are blamed for poor examination results and superiors are at fault for lack of promotions over the years. Whether true or not, such statements tend to reflect badly on you, suggesting that you are unable to face up to your shortcomings. If asked, admit your failings and show how you have tried to remedy them. Your endeavours will then come across as a strength, and be remembered more than the weaknesses.

Avoid becoming overconfident, and showing off to the interviewer. In particular, steer clear of dropping names left, right and centre. Comments such as 'Steve . . . he was my tutor at college' and 'Maureen . . . my old boss' make you sound silly and pretentious. Regaling your interviewer with amazing stories of how you and you alone saved the day for your previous employer appear equally ridiculous. Do not attempt to take over the interview so that you can talk endlessly about past glories, real or imagined. No one likes an arrogant bighead, and few will employ such a person.

Most important of all in your interview, do not worry. Always bear in mind that you are here on merit, invited in because the interviewer believes you have what it takes to do this job. You are probably one of the top six of perhaps hundreds of applicants, so you have absolutely no reason whatsoever to feel tense or inferior in any way. You know all there is to know about the organisation, yourself and the interview, and that you are the right person for the position. So why worry – you are going to be successful, and get that job!

2 THE OPENING MOMENTS

Arriving at the Organisation
Approaching the Interview Room
Listening to the Interviewer
Answering Preliminary Questions

2 THE OPENING MOMENTS

Having carried out all of your detailed preparatory work, you should be well prepared for your interview, whatever it is and whoever will be conducting it. Moving ahead, you now need to know about arriving at the organisation, approaching the interview room, listening to the interviewer and answering his or her preliminary questions. These first few moments are a crucially important time, during which you should be seeking to convey a strong, favourable impression and to set the scene for the coming thirty minutes or so.

ARRIVING AT THE ORGANISATION

Obviously, your first priority has to be to arrive for the interview, and you will have checked the date, time and place and conducted a trial run in advance to make certain that you will get there on time, ready for the appointment. If you allowed extra travelling time in case of mishaps and reach the premises with perhaps fifteen or more minutes to spare, take a walk around the block or find somewhere to sit and read a newspaper for ten minutes or so. Go in with about five minutes left. Should you expect to be delayed at all, telephone the organisation as soon as you can, leaving an explanatory and apologetic message for the interviewer and telling him or her when you expect to arrive. Although any delay is regrettable, letting your interviewer know in advance will limit the damage done as far as possible.

What happens when you enter the premises will depend upon the organisation, although hopefully you shall already have a good idea of what to expect if you paid a visit when conducting your research. Ideally, you will be greeted by a polite and friendly receptionist who knows who you are, is ready to deal with your expenses if appropriate and will then take you to a pleasant waiting area where you can hang up your overcoat, leave your baggage and sit down. He or she should offer you a tea or coffee and announce your arrival to the interviewer. At the other extreme, you may find an empty reception, have to search for help and be dealt with by bored staff who have no idea what you are talking about, and could not care less.

If you come face to face with an efficient receptionist, take the opportunity to chat to him or her whilst you are confirming who you are, the time of your appointment and attending to your expenses. It is helpful to find out what the interviewer looks like and whether he or she will come to meet you, so that you can be ready with a greeting. It is also worthwhile trying to pick up any extra snippets of information that might be useful to you at some stage. For example, the receptionist may comment that the interviews are running late because the interviewer's car was held up in traffic on the new ring road. Again, such a detail may be helpful later on when you meet, and are making small talk.

When guided to a waiting area, unload any heavy and cumbersome coat and bags. If you are offered a drink, decline it politely. You may not have time to finish it and even if you do, there are other last-minute tasks to tackle which are more important. Check your clothes, making sure that blouse buttons are fastened, flies are up, and whatever. Adjust your clothing as far as you can. Should you carry a small mirror, glance at your hair, eyes, nose, mouth and teeth for dandruff, smudged eyeliner and so on, as appropriate. Remedy your appearance as far as possible. This is your final chance.

Then take the opportunity to look quickly through any research material you have accumulated and brought with you, such as a sales brochure, the job description, the employee specification, photocopies of your application form or curriculum vitae and various jottings. Mull over what you have discovered about the organisation, the job and the type of person required. Think about your personality, strengths and weaknesses and what you are going to say about yourself to win that job. Imagine the interview, interviewer and the types of question you will have to answer, and recall the do's and don'ts of interviewing success.

Do try to relax, attempting to take it easy by breathing deeply and counting under your breath. Prepare a greeting such as 'Hello, Mrs Brownlow, I'm Neil Hicks. Pleased to meet you,' so that you know what you are going to say, instead of standing there speechless or blurting out a nonsensical word or phrase such as 'Goodnight' or 'Hello, where are you?' as some stressed interviewees have been known to do. Avoid repeating the greeting endlessly, though, as it tends to come out back to front when you eventually say it. 'Hello, Mrs Hicks, I'm Neil Brownlow' and so forth will simply highlight your nervousness. Always remember that you are here on merit, and are a winner. You have no reason to feel uptight or second-rate.

APPROACHING THE INTERVIEW ROOM

Within a few minutes, your interview will be due to begin, and you may then be sent along to the interview room alone as directed by the receptionist, could be taken there by him or her, or might even be met personally by the interviewer who has come out of the room to greet you. If you are expected to make your own way there, be absolutely certain that you know exactly where the interview room is. Hopefully, the directions given to you will be clear, such as 'If you'd like to go to the top of the stairs and through the swing doors, you'll find it's the third room on your left.' If you do not hear what the receptionist says or the instructions are complicated, ask him or her to repeat them. This is preferable to walking into a broom cupboard or disappearing for ten minutes as you stumble from one room to another.

Should the interview room be some distance from reception and the receptionist or another staff member is free, you might expect to be guided there in person. Be ready to make small talk as you travel up in a lift, walk along corridors, or whatever. The receptionist may ask if you had a good journey, found the premises easily or know the area at all. At the very least, you will probably have to exchange a few pleasantries about the weather. Recognise any questions and comments for what they are – a relatively painless way of passing the time, rather than standing or walking along in embarrassed silence. Clearly, the receptionist is not really interested in your journey or the number of dark clouds in the sky, so do not launch into lengthy explanations. Just say enough to nudge the conversation on – and keep your voice active and loosened up – until arriving at the destination.

Alternatively, the interviewer will make the effort to come and meet you in reception – and you may (rightly) see this as a sign of a caring organisation and would-be employer. Be prepared for this possibility, making certain you are not so engrossed in your thoughts that he or she has to speak to you several times before you register his or her presence. Expect your interviewer to appear when or shortly after your appointment is due. Make sure that your overcoat and bags have been hung up or put aside and any research material has been tucked away by that time. You do not want to be struggling with a heavy coat or scattering armfuls of literature across the floor as you stand up to greet the interviewer.

Not surprisingly, you must tackle this first meeting as it comes. Ideally, you will get to your feet as and when you see the interviewer. He or she will then realise you are Stephen Reynolds, Amanda Jessop, or whoever, the next interviewee. Of course, this depends on you knowing what your interviewer looks like. If you are unsure, you could be bobbing up and down continually, making you appear and feel foolish. Even if the receptionist has told you that the interviewer is a short, dark-haired man, there is still a risk that an endless procession of lookalikes might be coming through reception at that time. If in doubt, remain seated, stay alert and wait for your interviewer to move purposefully towards you.

Then stand up, looking him or her in the eyes and smiling warmly. Be ready to follow the interviewer's lead. Typically, he or she may offer his or her hand. If so, shake it firmly to show that you are confident and in a familiar situation. Too weak, and you appear nervous or half-hearted. Too strong, and you might be viewed as aggressive. If the interviewer does not move to shake hands, keep yours by your side. It is important to bear in mind that handshaking is not as commonplace as it once was and some interviewers no longer do it when greeting interviewees. Others simply do not feel comfortable with the procedure, which is understandable when a slightly built woman meets a huge bear of a man.

Let your interviewer begin the conversation, probably with an enquiring 'Mr Greene? . . . I'm Edward Hollis, your interviewer . . . Please come with me . . .' or something similar. Respond along the lines of 'Yes . . . Pleased to meet you . . . Of course . . .' or whatever seems appropriate. Remember to speak clearly and firmly. If you use the interviewer's name, it is 'Mr Hollis' not 'Edward', which is too familiar and disrespectful. Should the interviewer seem hesitant and uncertain, you can help him or her by speaking first, with a 'Hello, Mr Hollis, I'm Kevin Greene, pleased to meet you.' Do not forget that your interviewer may be less experienced than you at interviews and could be grateful for any help offered to ease his or her embarrassment and first-time nerves.

Again, be willing and able to make pleasant conversation with your interviewer on the way to the interview room, mindful that anything said or asked is to break the ice and put you (or indeed him or her) at ease, rather than an overwhelming desire to know everything about the route that you took to arrive at the organisation. Keep your comments short and relatively neutral, showing the interviewer that you are more than capable of maintaining an amicable and superficial conversation as and when necessary. After all, this may be a task that you will have to do in this job, so it is wise to start proving you can handle it now.

What happens when you get to the door of the interview room depends upon how you reached it. If you are alone, you should knock and wait to be called in by the interviewer. Try not to turn your back on him or her as you enter and shut the door behind you, as this seems rude. Greet the interviewer as you would have done in reception. Should you be accompanied by a receptionist or other employee, he or she will probably knock on the door, take you in and introduce you. Thank him or her for showing you the way. Then turn, smile, be ready to shake hands and so on. Be polite to everyone at all times.

If you have been guided along by the interviewer, he or she will lead you in, announcing you to any fellow interviewers who are waiting there for you, if appropriate. Stay calm, looking at them in sequence, smiling, nodding and so forth. Give each one your individual and equal attention. If you are dealing with only one interviewer, you might continue your small talk by commenting on the view from a window, a painting on the wall, or whatever. Wait to be shown to your seat rather than sitting down uninvited as some interviewees do. This appears ill-mannered and if you sit in the wrong chair, could be very embarrassing, too.

LISTENING TO THE INTERVIEWER

Now you are seated in the correct chair, leaning forward and looking interested in what the interviewer has to say, the interview is about to move into its introductory stages. Your interviewer will take his or her seat, shuffle various papers including your application form or curriculum vitae into view, and be ready to begin. Stay calm and relaxed, feeling well prepared to follow his or her lead. It is likely that the interviewer – experienced or inexperienced – will start by raising several, gentle questions such as these:

– Would you like a cup of tea or coffee?
– Shall I tell you about this interview?
– Shall I talk about the organisation?

WOULD YOU LIKE A CUP OF TEA OR COFFEE?

This is a popular icebreaker of an opening question, giving both parties a few moments to take stock of each other, feel at ease and prepare themselves for the coming conversation. It is most often asked when your interviewer has just met you for the first time as you enter the room and/or if this is the only interview that morning or afternoon. It is less frequently used when the interviewer is facing perhaps six or more interviews back to back. He or she is unlikely to want to drink endless cups of tea or coffee one after another. 'Can I offer you a drink?' is the same question, but phrased in a different way. 'A drink' should be taken to mean tea or coffee.

As a general rule, your response to this question should be a standardised 'No, thank you, I've just had one.' To show you are polite and considerate – and able to speak fluently – you might add the phrase 'You go ahead, though, if you'd like to have one.' A cup of tea or coffee is an unnecessary distraction and a prospective embarrassment. You may have to wait for a secretary to bring it in, and are unable to begin talking freely until it has arrived. Both the interviewer and you might reach for the milk or sugar at the same time. You could feel self-conscious about drinking tea without milk, or about putting three or four sugars into your coffee. It may be embarrassing to slurp over a hot drink, or to try to answer a question when you have a mouthful of tea or coffee. At worst, you might even spill your drink or drop it in your lap.

Similar questions which could open your conversation may

include 'Would you like a sweet?' and 'Can I offer you a cigarette?' Decline that sweet with 'Not for me, thanks. You have one though.' Almost inevitably, that peppermint will be stubbornly difficult to remove from the packet offered to you by the interviewer. It may become even more hazardous once it is in your mouth, getting in the way, sticking to your teeth or choking you as you speak. If you are tempted to accept a sweet, imagine the unfortunate first-time interviewee who saw a fruit pastille shoot out of his mouth whilst he was talking and land on the desk in front of the interviewer. That could happen to you.

It is equally sensible to turn down the offer of a cigarette with a polite 'No, thank you,' although it is courteous to indicate that your interviewer should smoke if he or she wishes to. Once more, you may fumble over the proffered cigarette, might be unable to light it, could choke on it, or whatever. As significant, smoking is becoming an increasingly unpopular practice in workplaces nowadays so it would be unwise to draw attention to your habit which could count against you if this is a predominantly no-smoking organisation. If the job involves coming into contact with flammable goods or dealing with customers then a nonsmoker may be required to do the work. If you do not smoke, make a point of saying so: 'No, thanks, I don't smoke . . . but you go ahead if you want one.'

SHALL I TELL YOU ABOUT THIS INTERVIEW?
'Yes, please' ought to be your reply, perhaps followed with 'I'd like to know what we're going to cover.' It is useful to be familiar with the topics that will be dealt with and their order, so that you are aware of where the conversation is leading. Taking education, qualifications, training, previous employment and so on in turn is probably the most popular sequence of topics but is not the only approach that may be adopted by the interviewer. He or she may prefer to work through your completed application form or curriculum vitae, and you should be ready to answer questions within this framework, if necessary.

Of course, detailing the interview that lies ahead may well be as much for the interviewer's benefit as for your own. He or she might be nervous, could wish to clarify what's what and may simply want to start the conversation by talking about a familiar, easy-to-explain subject. This suits you, too. Whilst he or she is chatting about the interview, you have more time to soak up the surroundings and to feel more relaxed and at ease with the situation.

SHALL I TALK ABOUT THE ORGANISATION?

This is another favourite opening question from an interviewer who wants to move into the interview by discussing a topic which he or she is well aware of, and can talk about at length. It is tempting to see this question as a further chance to absorb the atmosphere and relax. Do not do this though. Here is a golden opportunity for you to show that you are well prepared and have researched the organisation thoroughly, which should impress the interviewer and mark you out as a quality interviewee. As your interviewer pauses, speak up, with a friendly 'Well, why don't I tell you about the business to show I've done my homework.'

Having studied the organisation and anticipated this question, you should be able to sort quickly through the facts and figures that you have uncovered about its structure, activities, marketplace, customers and rivals. Provide a brief summary of these topics to show the breadth of your research, rather than concentrating on just one subject which suggests limited efforts. Try to be relevant and avoid talking too much about what you have discovered. This will eventually bore the interviewer, and makes you appear to be a smart alec.

As an example, you might say something like this: 'The Grove Studio is owned and run by yourself and your wife, Mrs Howard. You take the photographs and Mrs Howard handles the administration and sales. You specialise in portrait and wedding photography, employing part-timers to photograph weddings for you on Saturdays. Most of your portrait customers come from Northwood although you cover all of the county for weddings. There are two other studios in the town – Bellamy's in Wadgate Road and Flashes in Generals Mews. The Grove Studio is the most successful. You've won several awards for your portraits including the trade association's Pet Photographer of the Year for 1992.' Succinct, extensive *and* flattering – what a winner!

ANSWERING PRELIMINARY QUESTIONS

Some interviewers prefer to press on with the conversation as soon as possible rather than talking about the interview or organisation. At the same time, they do not want to launch straight into asking tough questions about qualifications, previous employment or whatever, which may unsettle even the best interviewees. Hence, they begin by raising various easy-to-answer questions, such as these:

– When were you born?
– Where do you live?
– What do your parents do?
– What do they think about your application for this job?
– Tell me about yourself

WHEN WERE YOU BORN?
See this for what it is – a basic question which you can reply to quickly, without having to think through your answer. Your interviewer can inevitably see your date of birth on the application form or curriculum vitae, but just wants to get you chatting with as little hesitation and embarrassment as possible. Give a simple and straightforward response, perhaps, 'I was born on 7 September 1975, I'm eighteen next week.' A similar question such as 'Where were you born?' ought to produce a corresponding reply such as 'I was born at Worthsham Hospital, down in Sussex.' Whatever you do, never stare at your interviewer as though he or she is mad, and avoid saying something like

'That's on the form.' The interviewer is trying to help you, so do not reject his or her kind gesture.

WHERE DO YOU LIVE?
If your interviewer believes you look tense and nervous, he or she might ask you this question, possibly as an alternative or in addition to 'When were you born?' Again, a short response is sufficient, perhaps 'I live in Thomas Avenue, Trimley.' Add a little extra, though, to show you can maintain *and* develop a conversation. 'It's up on the new Beaumont Park estate. Do you know it?' might be appropriate. Be prepared for the interviewer exploring this further. For example, he or she might say 'How long have you lived there?' or 'Do you like that part of the town?'

Speaking clearly and staying to the point, elaborate upon your initial comment. 'We moved in during May – one of the first families to do so. It'll be nice up there when it's all finished. At the moment, the builders are still working away, so it's all a bit of a mess.' Alternatively, you could say 'Yes, we've lived on all three of the main housing estates over the past seven or eight years and I like this one most of all. We overlook a park, are close to the new supermarket and the bus stops opposite our house, so I can be in the town centre within five minutes of coming out of the front door!'

WHAT DO YOUR PARENTS DO?
This question is a popular one, often asked early on in the conversation to put younger applicants at ease, and to get to know them better. Unfortunately, it is sometimes misinterpreted by these interviewees, who regard it with suspicion as if the 'wrong' background will lose them the job, or simply as downright instrusive. They wonder what their parents have to do with their application. Do not become defensive or uptight about this innocuous, throwaway question. Just answer it, perhaps with 'Dad's just been made redundant from Thurlows

factory. As you may know it's closing down because of the recession. Mum's a cleaner at the Tower Ramparts Shopping Centre. She's supporting the family until Dad gets another job.'

A similar 'get to know you' question is 'Do you have any brothers or sisters?' Again, take this at face value and as an opportunity to chat and establish a rapport. You might say 'Yes, I've an older brother and a younger sister. Michael's twenty-one and at the University of East Anglia, training to be a primary school teacher. Sophie's sixteen and is doing GCSEs at Waybury High School this summer.' Be positive about your family, whatever they do. Try to indicate that you are proud of them and are happy together. After all, the interviewer may assume that if you cannot get on with your parents, brothers and sisters, you will not mix with your fellow employees. He or she may be correct.

WHAT DO THEY THINK ABOUT YOUR APPLICATION FOR THIS JOB?

Here, your interviewer is probing a little, building upon your answers to the questions about your parents, brothers or sisters to find out if your family are for or against the application. Not surprisingly, he or she is unlikely to choose you if you are at odds with your parents about the job. Parental pressure may affect your work or persuade you to leave in three or four months' time – which will be a blow to the organisation as it will have spent time and money settling you in. You could say 'They're all very supportive. Mum and Dad see this as a great opportunity to do a job I've always wanted to do at a go-ahead firm offering me plenty of opportunities for promotion if I do well.' If your parents are against this application, perhaps you are applying for the wrong job. It may be worthwhile reviewing your strengths and weaknesses once again.

TELL ME ABOUT YOURSELF

What a question! It is a tough one, thrown at you early on to see how you cope and whether you are able to give a lucid and relevant response. Your interviewer also wants to know how you view yourself to find out if you are an arrogant bighead or a sensible, level-headed person whom he or she would wish to employ. Do not panic when you hear this question. You are well prepared, in control and – most important of all – you know the answers from that earlier research. Think quickly about your personality and strengths, picking out those qualities which show that you are well matched to the organisation and job, and are the ideal employee waiting to be recruited.

This is what you might say: 'Well, I'm eighteen years old. I've six GCSEs, including art, craft, design and technology, and maths and computer studies, all at A grades. I received Bs for English language and English literature. I'm a hard-working person who'll tackle any task he's asked to do. I'm friendly, too, and make an effort to get on with everyone around me. I'm ambitious as well – I want to learn a trade, and progress with an equally ambitious company. I've always wanted to be a printer for as long as I can recall – which is why I'm sitting here today, applying to be a trainee with you!'

THE OPENING MOMENTS: AN ACTION CHECKLIST

It can be a good idea to sketch out some of the points you want to make in response to these questions. Don't rehearse your replies in a parrot fashion though – they will sound stilted and odd, especially if the questions are phrased in a different way than expected.

Would you like a cup of tea or coffee?

Where do you live?

Shall I tell you about this interview?

What do your parents do?

Shall I talk about the organisation?

What do they think about your application for this job?

When were you born?

Tell me about yourself

3 EDUCATION, QUALIFICATIONS AND TRAINING

Focusing on Your Education
Examining Your Qualifications
Talking About Training

3 EDUCATION, QUALIFICATIONS AND TRAINING

When it becomes clear to the interviewer that you are starting to relax and a rapport is developing, he or she will move on to ask you serious, probing questions to discover if you are the right person for this job. Typically, the interviewer will begin this quesioning by focusing on your education, subsequently examining your qualifications and talking about training, in turn. Obviously, the importance attached to these topics will vary according to your circumstances – a young person with little or no work experience must expect the interviewer to concentrate fully upon them, whereas an older person may receive only a superficial assessment of his or her academic abilities and achievements.

FOCUSING ON YOUR EDUCATION

Questions about your education will almost certainly feature early on in the interview, whether the interviewer takes the popular education–qualifications–training–employment route or prefers to work through your application form or curriculum vitae in chronological order. It is most likely that your interviewer will focus exclusively upon the last educational establishment that you attended – school, college or university, as appropriate. Hence, you may need to mentally amend the following questions from 'school' to 'college' or 'university', whichever applies to your individual circumstances:

51

- Which school did you attend?
- Why did you go to that school?
- What did you like about your school?
- What did you dislike about your school?
- What was your favourite subject?
- What was your least-liked subject?
- What else did you do at school, apart from studying?
- What did you do during your holidays?

WHICH SCHOOL DID YOU ATTEND?

In many ways, this is a comparable question to 'When were you born?' and 'Where do you live?' It is a simple, fact-checking question asked as much to start you talking as anything else. Give a straight answer: 'I went to Stonham High School', 'I'm still at Wesbury College', or whatever. Add a little extra comment, again to show that you are able to converse confidently, perhaps 'I was there for five years, from September '87 to June '92,' or 'I'm due to leave after my exams in June.' Avoid making references to the application form or curriculum vitae which contains this information, as such comments appear ill-mannered. Do not throw the interviewer's considerate gesture back into his or her face.

WHY DID YOU GO TO THAT SCHOOL?

Not as daft a question as it sounds and worthy of a better answer than the shrugged 'Dunno' or 'Cos I did' that some younger interviewees have been known to give. If the interviewer can see from your application form that you live some way from your school, then he or she may want to know why you went there, instead of a local one. Even if you attended a nearby school, a choice of perhaps two might exist and he or she could wish to find out why this one was selected in preference to the other.

Residing some distance from the school, you might say 'I went there because we lived near it when I was eleven. When we moved to Woodleigh the year before last, I carried on at Thretford High as a change might have affected my GCSEs.' Clearly, this is a sensible answer, showing that you are dedicated to your work and conscientious, which are both qualities that are likely to appeal to a would-be employer. Having made a choice between two schools, you could say, 'Well, my parents selected this school for me because I was only eleven at the time. They thought it would be better than Ablett High as the classes were smaller, facilities were newer and the exam results were superior. I think they were right.' Obviously, if you chose your college or university you would state this, and then explain your reasons in the same way.

WHAT DID YOU LIKE ABOUT YOUR SCHOOL?

Here your interviewer is probing to find out more about you and your likes, to see if you are the best person for the job. Think for a moment about the attributes that he or she is looking for. Perhaps these were stated on the employee specification that you obtained from the organisation, or possibly you worked them out for yourself by studying the job and the work involved with it. 'Hard-working', 'ambitious', 'able to show initiative', 'mature' – these and other phrases may spring readily to mind. Provide the interviewer with an answer which suggests that you have these qualities – and in abundance.

This would be a winning response showing that you are 'hard-working' and 'able to show initiative'. 'Oh, many things. It was a good school. The teachers were great – they were always available at lunchtimes and after school to help me with the work I was doing. My history teacher even came round to my house during the Easter holidays to look at a project I'd been working on for my GCSE.' Whatever you say, avoid the jokey response that many naive interviewees give. 'Lunchtimes!, 'The bell at the end of the day!' or 'The holidays!' are all (well-worn) answers that are not remotely funny in an interview, and only succeed in making you look foolish. Nobody will employ a fool.

WHAT DID YOU DISLIKE ABOUT YOUR SCHOOL?

A similar question which should not be answered with a (so-called) humorous aside such as 'The work!' or the rather rude and sullen 'What didn't I dislike about it?' Your interviewer wants a properly thought-out reply which will enable him or her to assess your suitability to the job, so provide that answer. You might stress that you are 'ambitious' and 'mature' by saying something like this: 'I think the class sizes in the last couple of years were rather large and the teachers were unable to give pupils their individual attention during lessons. To get on, you had to approach them out of class. To be fair, the teachers always helped you out of hours, when you asked them for assistance.'

Do be especially careful to avoid being critical when answering this question. It is tempting to moan about the school, the teacher who did not seem to like you and the vagaries of the education system, particularly if the interviewer seems sympathetic. Remember that such criticisms can and do backfire whether or not they are valid, making you appear as a whining no-hoper. Similarly, steer clear of saying too much. It is easy to drone on and on about this subject, boring the interviewer with your views. Likewise, do not be irrelevant. The fact that second helpings were never available at lunchtimes or the custard was always lumpy is of no interest to anyone – and commenting on such trivial matters makes you look very silly indeed.

WHAT WAS YOUR FAVOURITE SUBJECT?

Again, your interviewer is trying to probe, to find out what you are like as a person. Clearly, it is sensible to refer to a subject which has some bearing on the job, perhaps typing if you are applying to a be a secretary or business studies if you wish to become a trainee manager. Hopefully, your favourite subject will also be one of your best ones, as reflected in your examination grades. Explain why you liked it so much, preferably touching upon your qualities for the job, where possible.

Needless to state, you should not say that you enjoyed it because the teacher did not make you do any work, or had a nervous twitch which made the class laugh.

Applying for a post as a trainee manager, you could say: 'Business studies. I really enjoyed that – it gave me a good introduction to the theory and practice of business management. Our teacher encouraged us to work on projects in small groups. Three of us put together a business plan for a new, small concern. We then took it to the local bank. Their small business adviser discussed it with us – and said she'd lend us the money! I seemed to be able to grasp this subject particularly quickly and was really pleased to learn I received an A grade for it in my exams.'

WHAT WAS YOUR LEAST-LIKED SUBJECT?

Another probing question which needs some thought before you reply to it. The safest response is probably to indicate that you least enjoyed a subject which was less relevant to what you want to do – biology for a typist, chemistry for a bank clerk, or whatever. Do not say or imply that you disliked it because the teacher was awful at his job or the work was too hard, which will not impress a prospective employer. Similarly, avoid suggesting that you did not try as hard as you did in your favourite subject, as this indicates you might adopt a comparable attitude towards the less enjoyable aspects of the job you have applied for. Say that you did your best, supporting this comment by referring to a reasonable examination grade if you can.

A would-be typist might say: 'Well, I think I enjoyed most of the subjects I studied at school. None of them stand out as being really dreadful. I suppose if I had to choose one, I'd say biology but only because it isn't as relevant to what I want to do as others are. There's not much call for dissecting worms in an office, is there! I had a go, though, and received a B grade in my GCSE which I was pleased with.' This is a good, play-safe response.

WHAT ELSE DID YOU DO AT SCHOOL, APART FROM STUDYING?

This – or more direct questions such as 'What did you achieve at school?', 'Were you a prefect?' and 'Did you play for any school teams?' – will almost inevitably be raised when talking about your time at school, or college or university, as appropriate. Not surprisingly, the interviewer is trying to build up a fuller picture of you. He or she wants to know if you are a robot who does nothing but study, or whether you have any other interests. If you do, he or she wishes to discover what these tell him or her about you. Perhaps the prefect is a natural leader, the hockey player a good team person, and so on.

Knowing your qualities and strengths – and how valuable that background research is now proving to be – you can give an answer which shows how well suited you are to the job. 'I spent a lot of time in the evenings helping to put on end-of-term stage shows. As you may know, Norwood has a good reputation locally for quality productions – they always play to packed houses. I worked as part of the backstage team, doing whatever was needed – painting the scenery, aiming spotlights, making tea . . . just about everything, really.' If the interviewer wants a hard-working all-rounder, he or she has found one!

WHAT DID YOU DO DURING YOUR HOLIDAYS?

A follow-up question to 'What else did you do at school, apart from studying?', and asked for the same reasons. Indicate that you did something which proves you have one or more of the qualities needed for the job. Perhaps the interviewer is seeking an employee who can take instructions, works as part of a team and is friendly and helpful. Thus, 'In the last holidays I helped the leaders of the local Brownie pack to take them all on summer camp. It was hard work but great fun – cooking, lighting fires, leading singalongs, settling squabbles and mopping up tears. You name it – I did it!' Similar questions such as 'What do you do in the evenings?' and 'What do you do at weekends?' should be answered in the same manner, linking your activities to the requirements of the job.

EXAMINING YOUR QUALIFICATIONS

With a fuller understanding of your education, the interviewer will then move on effortlessly towards the qualifications that you achieved – or did not achieve – during your time at school, college or university, as relevant. Various questions may be asked, of which the following ones are very popular:

- What qualifications do you have?
- Why did you choose to study those subjects?
- What do you think of your results?
- If you could choose again, would you study the same subjects?
- How well do you expect to do?
- Are qualifications important?

WHAT QUALIFICATIONS DO YOU HAVE?

Your immediate reaction to this question may be that it is pointless – the information was stated on the application form or curriculum vitae that you completed and which now lies on the desk in front of the interviewer. He or she can see your list of qualifications simply by turning the page. Having spent a few minutes conversing, you are calm and relaxed so your interviewer no longer needs to continue feeding you with simple, easy-to-answer questions. You might even feel that he or she is patronising you, especially if you are rather sensitive about your qualifications because they are not as good as you would like them to be.

Think carefully before replying, though, particularly if you are tempted to give a blunt response which will lose you the job. The question is a valid one, often used as a stepping stone by the interviewer to move on from a general discussion about your

FOCUSING ON YOUR EDUCATION: AN ACTION CHECKLIST

Think carefully about your replies to the following questions and jot down the key points you want to put across to your interviewer. This will help to gather together your thoughts.

Which school did you attend?

What was your favourite subject?

Why did you go to that school?

What was your least-liked subject?

What did you like about your school?

What else did you do at school, apart from studying?

What did you dislike about your school?

What did you do during your holidays?

education to a specific look at your qualifications. Also, your interviewer may not really know what qualifications you possess. Brought up in the days of O levels, A levels and degrees, he or she might not be familiar with BTEC, RSA, NVQs, CPVEs, HNDs and the like. What the interviewer could be saying is 'What the heck is a BTEC HND in business and finance?'

Give a brief reply, demystifying jargon *and* highlighting your strengths for the post. For example, 'I've eight GCSEs, three A levels in business studies, French and German all at C grades, and a BTEC Higher National Diploma in business and finance. That's a two-year course run by the Business and Technology Education Council which is the equivalent of a basic degree but deals with business practice more than with theory. We spent a lot of time preparing projects and working in industry.' A spot-on answer – clear, understandable and stressing business and language qualifications which were mentioned in the advertisement for the job vacancy.

WHY DID YOU CHOOSE TO STUDY THOSE SUBJECTS?

Now your interviewer is trying to find out more about you, to see whether your examination subjects were chosen with this type of job in mind, or if you made a haphazard selection not knowing what you wanted to do after your studies. Clearly, he or she is looking for you to confirm that your choice was part of an overall plan building up to this job. Hopefully, you can do this: 'I've always been interested in sports for as long as I can remember and have wanted to work in a leisure centre since before my GCSEs. After I passed these, I had a choice of studying for A levels or a National Certificate in leisure studies, which combined business management and sports-related subjects. This seemed ideal as the idea of becoming a trainee manager at a leisure centre was really appealing. So here I am, applying for that job!'

Of course, you may have made a random selection because you really did not know what you wanted to do, choosing to study art, biology and geography at A level and then applying to be a sales representative. Alternatively, you could have made a particular choice as you had mapped out your future but then changed your mind, studying for a diploma in secretarial studies and consequently applying to be a shop assistant. Tell the truth about your reasons. After all, it is not surprising that young people do not know what they wish to do for the next forty years or so, nor is it unexpected that they change their minds. It is a big decision. Try to indicate that you have decided now, though – and want this job!

This is what you might say: 'To be frank, I really didn't know what I wanted to do when I was sixteen – I don't think many people do if they're absolutely honest. Anyway, I chose art, biology and geography because I felt they'd give me a broad spread of experiences for whatever I eventually decided to do. I was good at them, too – I got two As and a B. It wasn't until towards the end of my studies that I decided I wanted to become a sales representative. Perhaps they weren't the best subjects for this job, but I did learn a lot from them.' You are honest *and* positive about this job – a winning reply!

As an alternative: 'I studied for a secretarial studies diploma because I thought I wanted to be a secretary after leaving school. I spent a year learning how to be a secretary and working for various firms as part of my course. To be honest, I didn't enjoy being stuck in an office from nine till five doing the same tasks over and over again. I had a Saturday job at Worleys, the big department store in Whittleby, and loved every minute of it – helping in the storeroom, unpacking and displaying goods, meeting different people all the time. I changed my mind – shop work's for me.' Again, such truthfulness and enthusiasm make this a successful response.

WHAT DO YOU THINK OF YOUR RESULTS?

A popular question which crops up in many interviews albeit in different guises – 'To what would you attribute your success?', 'Why were your exam results so poor?', 'Could you have done better in your exams?', 'Do your qualifications reflect your abilities?' and so on. The interviewer is trying to discover how you see yourself, in an attempt to piece together a broader picture of you. He or she probably wants to find out how mature you are, and whether you are able to take a balanced view of your results, or if you boast or blame others, as appropriate. If you did well, be modest, acknowledging those who helped you to be a winner. If you did badly, be honest, recognising the reasons for your shortcomings. Whatever you say, try to show your strengths for the job as well, difficult though this may seem to be.

As an example, if you achieved quality results, you might say something along the lines of 'I was very happy with them. I worked hard, got a lot of help from my teachers and was fortunate enough to receive good grades. I was especially pleased with my maths and English language A grades and statistics B grade. I found this a difficult subject to grasp at first and had to work extra hard to master it fully.' Modest, suitably qualified and an exceptionally hard worker at difficult tasks – what more could the interviewer want!

Perhaps you were not so successful and need to face up to this fact, taking responsibility for your own weaknesses instead of lashing out at everything and everyone else. 'To be truthful, I wasn't satisfied with them. My grades for history, geography, English literature and English language were fine, but failing maths, French and physics was a disappointment. I think I concentrated too much on my good subjects and hoped for the best with the other ones, which was foolish. I should have given equal attention to all of them. Still, I'm going to study maths and French at night school from September and I'll make sure I do well this time. I'll not make the same mistake twice.'

IF YOU COULD CHOOSE AGAIN, WOULD YOU STUDY THE SAME SUBJECTS?

Another probing question from your interviewer often asked as a follow-up to the previous two questions if you made an unsuitable choice of subjects or obtained poor grades. See this as an opportunity to build upon your last two answers and convince the interviewer that you are the right person for the job. Having conducted your research into the organisation, job and type of person required, you should know what subjects you ought to have studied. Knowing yourself well and where you went wrong, you will also be aware of what you should have done to have got it right. Thus, you ought to be able to give the right answer, according to your individual circumstances.

Your reply could be as follows: 'No, I increased my knowledge and experiences in many ways by doing art, biology and geography, but I don't think they are the most appropriate A levels for a sales representative to have. Now that I know what I really want to do, I'd choose business studies plus French and German, especially for a go-ahead firm such as yours which is expanding into Europe. I've actually applied to the adult education centre at Southburgh College to see if I can study business studies and French A levels at evening classes from September – make up for lost time!'

Alternatively, your response may be something like this: 'No, in retrospect I'd have gone to college and studied for a National Diploma in retail studies which would have given me a fuller introduction to how shops are managed and run. Still, having secretarial skills will always stand me in good stead. Typing is a useful skill to have. I'm also now doing a correspondence course in retailing through the Open University. This covers the same topics as the National Diploma, and is just as detailed, if not more so.'

HOW WELL DO YOU EXPECT TO DO?

You may be attending an interview before your examination results are known. If so, then this question is certain to arise if various qualifications and grades are considered to be essential or desirable for the job. Having done your homework, you should be able to give a positive reply, focusing on those qualifications which were referred to in the recruitment advertisement and employee specification, and promoting your other relevant qualities too. 'I hope to do well. I worked hard in all subjects, especially maths and English which are very important. I received lots of support from my teachers and with a little luck, I should get good grades.' Needless to state, do not be a braggart. Boasting that you will receive A's in this, that and the other will make you appear arrogant – and unemployable.

WHY DO YOU NOT WANT TO GO ON TO FURTHER EDUCATION?

A valid question which is likely to be asked of a school or college leaver, especially one who has achieved good enough results to go on to do A levels or a degree, but who chooses not to do so. The interviewer wishes to know why, to find out what makes you tick and what the thinking is behind your decision. To impress, your reply must show that you have thought carefully about this, weighed up the alternatives and reached the logical *and* correct conclusion. For example, 'Well, I considered the choices and felt that I already had the qualifications needed to obtain this job, which is what I've always wanted to do. I don't think A levels would help me to do the work any better. I'm keen to keep learning, though, both on the job and by studying for professional exams as I progress, perhaps in the evenings.'

ARE QUALIFICATIONS IMPORTANT?

What a question! This can – and frequently does – leave unprepared interviewees speechless or floundering around for something to say. Do not panic, though – it is not as tough as it sounds. The interviewer and you must both realise that the importance of qualifications has to vary according to a particular job, so perhaps he or she is really saying 'Are qualifications important for this job?' Thus, your answer is relatively easy to give, *if* you have done your preliminary work and found out whether qualifications figure prominently in the job advertisement and employee specification, or not.

Here is a typical, solid reply: 'I believe the importance of qualifications really depends on the type of job. Generally speaking,

I'd say that qualifications can often give you the basic, theoretical knowledge of a subject which can then be built upon through on-the-job training and experience. For this job as an office junior, I think my maths and English GCSEs provide me with the basic skills required for office life, but I still have a lot to learn about the practicalities which I'll pick up on a day-to-day basis.' With this sensible, balanced response, you should meet with the interviewer's approval.

TALKING ABOUT TRAINING

Questions about the training you have had for this post fall somewhere between the topics of qualifications and previous employment, since any training received may have led to qualifications or could have been built into your last job. Nevertheless, it is likely to be covered in some capacity, and could be dealt with separately in some instances, with questions such as:

- What training have you had?
- Why did you do that training?
- What did you think of the training?
- How might it have been improved?
- How have you benefited from that training?

WHAT TRAINING HAVE YOU HAD?

A simple question, asked by the interviewer who is keen to learn more about the skills, knowledge and experience that you would bring to the organisation and job. Give a straightforward answer, referring to any *relevant* training you have had and explaining it in a concise manner. 'In my last term at school, all of the leavers went out to work in various jobs and organisations for two weeks. Knowing that I wanted to be a journalist, I spent a fortnight at the *Evening Echo*. I spent a couple of days working in each of the departments there, to get to know the ropes, and

EXAMINING QUALIFICATIONS: AN ACTION CHECKLIST

Write down the points you want to put over in reply to these questions about your qualifications. Having an idea of what you will say will be of great benefit to you when these questions arise.

What qualifications do you have?

How well do you expect to do?

Why did you choose to study those subjects?

Why do you not want to go on to further education?

What do you think of your results?

Are qualifications important?

If you could choose again, would you study the same subjects?

to learn how a newspaper was produced. It was very informative.'

WHY DID YOU DO THAT TRAINING?

This is virtually the same question as 'Why did you choose to study those subjects?' which you faced when talking about your qualifications. Once more, your interviewer is trying to spot a sense of purpose and a clear-minded determination to work towards this job. Thus, a winning reply might be along the lines of 'I did it because I believed it would increase my skills and knowledge in this field, help me to get this job *and* do it better than I would otherwise have done.' Avoid answers such as 'I was told to do it by my class tutor' or 'Because the job centre said I'd lose my benefit if I didn't go on it.' These will not impress the interviewer at all, and will blow your chances of success.

WHAT DID YOU THINK OF THE TRAINING?

By raising this question, the interviewer is building up a fuller picture of you in two ways. What you say about the training will help him or her to decide if it really is as relevant to the organisation and job as you are suggesting. Also, the way in which you talk about it will tell him or her more about you as a person. You may give a balanced assessment, generally being upbeat about it, or you might moan and groan, criticising everything left, right and centre. To succeed, mix together a level-headed appraisal of your training with a dash of enthusiasm for its positive aspects.

Here is what you might say to the interviewer: 'All in all, it was very worthwhile. Short though the course was, it gave me a solid introduction to maintaining all types of cars. Beforehand, I could repair my own car, which is a Fiesta, but that was about it. During the course we worked on a wide range of vehicles and although they were mainly older ones I now feel confident that I could deal with problems on most cars, whether a Mini or a Rover, a Skoda or a Jaguar. It's given me the grounding to become a good mechanic.'

68

HOW MIGHT IT HAVE BEEN IMPROVED?

Pressing on, the interviewer is giving you a second chance to elaborate on your training, and for the same reasons. It is another opportunity for you either to show how mature and well balanced you are *or* to lose the job altogether by giving a critical, whining response. Of course, there were shortcomings but you made the best of them – as you will do with the less pleasant aspects of this post. 'I think the course had some teething troubles because it was the first time it had been run, so one or two difficulties should be expected. In future, I believe the organisers are going to add on an extra couple of days which would be useful. Overall, I thought the course was good, and a great help to me.'

HOW HAVE YOU BENEFITED FROM THAT TRAINING?

Another probing question, and a glorious invitation for you to hammer home the key skills, knowledge and experience which you will bring to this job if chosen. You know what the interviewer wants from the ideal employee and you are aware of what you can offer. Being brief and to the point, fire back a winning answer – and get that job! 'Oh, in many ways. It taught me how to bake bread, cakes and biscuits – and attractive and edible ones, too! As significant, I learned a lot about the theory as well – how an oven works, how to make best use of it, the importance of hygiene and being seen to be clean, how to handle customers and so on. Prior to this training, I knew I wanted to be a successful baker; now I know how to become one.'

TALKING ABOUT TRAINING: AN ACTION CHECKLIST

Mull over your answers to these questions and put down the main points that you want to talk about in the interview.

What training have you had?

Why did you do that training?

What did you think of the training?

How might it have been improved?

How have you benefited from that training?

4 EMPLOYMENT ISSUES

Discussing Previous Employment
Viewing This Vacancy
Contemplating Future Employment

4 EMPLOYMENT ISSUES

Having questioned you about your education, qualifications and training, your interviewer is then likely to lead you on towards various employment issues which need to be covered in some detail, whether you have worked before or not. He or she will probably want to discuss your previous employment if appropriate, discover your views about this particular vacancy and find out how you contemplate your future employment in the marketplace. Experienced or inexperienced in this field, much of the interview will revolve around work-related matters.

DISCUSSING PREVIOUS EMPLOYMENT

Now well into the interview, your interviewer will be pushing hard to learn all he or she can about your personality, strengths and weaknesses to see if you are suited to the organisation and job. He or she will wish to talk through your previous jobs, possibly concentrating on the most recent one you have had, or still have, as relevant. Even if you are a younger interviewee who has just left school, college or university, probing questions will be asked about any part-time or holiday jobs you have held. Popular questions include these ones:

- Tell me about your last job
- What did you like about the job?
- What did you dislike about the job?
- What problems did you have to deal with?
- How did you handle that task?

- What have you learned from that job?
- What did you think of your boss?
- How did you get that job?
- How long did you do that job?
- Why did you hold that job for such a short time?
- Why have you had so many jobs?
- Why have you had that job for such a long time?
- Why did you leave your last job?

TELL ME ABOUT YOUR LAST JOB

This question crops up in almost all interviews, albeit in different guises. 'Describe a typical day in your last job' or 'What were the main responsibilities and tasks of your old job?' might be posed instead. However it is phrased, the interviewer is simply trying to compare your previous job with the one you have applied for to find out whether you have accumulated the necessary skills, knowledge and experience required to do this work properly. Having researched the job thoroughly by studying the job description, talking to the outgoing employee and so on, and having contemplated your strengths, you should find this an easy one to answer. You just pick out and refer to the main similarities between the two jobs.

For example, you may say to your interviewer, 'In many ways, it is very comparable with this job. I worked four days on, four off, four nights on, four off, and so forth, which got me used to working shift patterns. I was in charge of security for a similar-sized complex to this one and supervised a team of five other guards as in this post. Much of the job involved being seen, so as well as checking doors, security and alarm systems regularly and watching out for thieves and burglars, we had to make sure that we kept a high profile both in and out of office hours, simply by walking around. It certainly kept me very fit indeed!'

WHAT DID YOU LIKE ABOUT THE JOB?

Here, your interviewer is investigating further, probing behind your initial comments to discover more about the job. At the same time, he or she wants to learn about you, and your attitude to work. The interviewer wishes to know whether you just like the easiest or most glamorous parts of the job, or if you are pre-pared to take the rough with the smooth, the mundane with the exciting, and so on. Invariably, the interviewer is looking to re-cruit someone with a positive attitude towards work, and who is willing to tackle messy or boring chores with enthusiasm and vigour.

Therefore, your reply should be something along these lines: 'Overall, I liked my job as a librarian at Pendlebury library very much. My two years there coincided with a time of great change and I particularly enjoyed being involved with the introduction of the computerised system for monitoring books and the build-ing of a new romantic fiction section, which proved to be very popular. I also enjoyed talking to people, helping them to find the books they wanted, assisting schoolchildren with projects and so forth. Of course there was a down side – asking noisy teenagers to be quiet, chasing up overdue books and the like, but all in all it was a very happy and worthwhile time. I felt I was at the hub of the community, and playing my part within it.'

WHAT DID YOU DISLIKE ABOUT THE JOB?
A similar question to the last one, probably raised because your previous reply concentrated too much on the more pleasant aspects of your job. You are being given a second chance – so take it! Provide a well-balanced answer, showing a mature atti-tude and a willingness to approach *all* tasks with equal effort. 'Well I guess that working in a pet shop can be a messy job at times – I had to clean out the cages, which wasn't very pleasant, but then that's part and parcel of the job. You've got to take the good with the bad, and at the end of the day, it was a great job for someone who loves working with animals.'

WHAT PROBLEMS DID YOU HAVE TO DEAL WITH?
With this question, the interviewer is really pressing hard to un-cover what the job was like, to match it up with the one he or

she is trying to fill. Draw on your extensive accumulated knowledge, and select those difficulties which occurred in your last job *and* that are likely to crop up in this post, too. Comment on them – whilst making it very clear that you were happy to handle them, because they were part of the job which you enjoyed doing through pleasant *and* unpleasant times. 'Stock deliveries from suppliers were the big problem – they were inevitably late, which meant constant 'phone calls to the manufacturers and to customers who were waiting for the goods. I was responsible for those calls and although some were hard, I was pleased to do them. It taught me a lot about talking to people, in all situations.'

HOW DID YOU HANDLE THAT TASK?

Picking up on one of the problems you mentioned, your interviewer will probably say 'How did you deal with late deliveries?', 'How did you handle these customers?', or whatever. He or she wants to assess whether these unfortunate experiences toughened you up, and gave you the necessary knowledge and skills to make a success this time around. Explain what you did – and win this job! 'I'd draw up a list of waiting customers from the order book and call them to apologise, explain what had happened and tell them when the goods were due to arrive, promising to chase these up. I'd always allow a few extra days for delivery just in case! I'd then ring them back when the goods had arrived, to arrange delivery. This time, the goods would seem to have arrived early because I'd chased them up for the customers, so they'd be really pleased. This way, I'd turn angry customers into happy ones!'

WHAT HAVE YOU LEARNED FROM THAT JOB?

Here is your chance to take an overall view of that last job and to give the interviewer what he or she wants – a summary of the skills, knowledge and experience that developed from it to make you the best person for this job. This is how you might reply: 'I learned an enormous amount in my two years at the toy shop. I

know how a retail outlet operates, how to display goods effectively, and how to use a till and a computer terminal. I can negotiate with manufacturers and wholesalers, place orders with sales
representatives and sell to customers on a face-to-face basis. I
knew nothing about this until I joined Kaleidoscope, and learned
so much from everyone there in a relatively short space of time.'

WHAT DID YOU THINK OF YOUR BOSS?

'Did you like your boss?', 'Did you get on with your boss?',
'What did you think of your colleagues?', 'Did you mix well
with your colleagues?' and so on – all of these questions are
essentially the same as 'What did you think of your boss?' They
are asked by the interviewer who wants to take on someone who
will fit into a team system, get along with everyone and not be a
disruptive troublemaker. Thus, your answer to this and similar
questions must be positive, showing the interviewer that you are
that person. Remember to avoid being critical – whatever the
rights or wrongs of the matter, criticism tends to reflect badly on
you. Steer clear of it.

If your former employer was a first-class boss, you might say
something like 'Mrs Allenby was a great person to work for.
Although she was very much in charge, she encouraged us to
raise ideas and make suggestions about the work before reaching
any decisions. She listened to what we had to say and took on
board our comments, which made us feel we were contributing
to the department's success. Also, she always credited ideas to
whoever raised them rather than taking the glory for herself, so
she had the respect of the whole department.' When talking
about a boss, do not forget to say 'Mrs Allenby' rather than
'Patricia', 'Pat', 'Pattie' or any other overfamiliar name. Show
your respect, by keeping your distance.

Perhaps you think your boss was a dreadful person to work
for. Nevertheless, you must have learned something from him
or her which will be helpful in the future – even if it is how not
to be a boss! Take this answer as an example of what you could
say in these circumstances. 'Mr Boden was a good boss to have –

I discovered a lot whilst I worked for him. He adopted a *laissez-faire* approach to management and delegated many responsibilities to his team. This gave me the chance to use my initiative, take decisions for myself, and learn from my successes and failures. It was a very beneficial period of time for me.'

HOW DID YOU GET THAT JOB?

Quite simply, your interviewer is looking for signs of initiative which may be considered to be an essential requirement for this job. As a successful job hunter on a previous occasion, you must have done something out of the ordinary to have been a winner. Tell the interviewer what it was – and show that initiative! 'Well, I went through the usual process of reading the advertisement, sending in my CV and attending an interview before being offered the job. I like to think I got it by showing initiative and always being one step ahead of the rest. There's a tour around the local weekly newspaper as it's being printed – I went on that and saw the advert before anyone else. Then I faxed my CV through so that it was the first to arrive. Before the interview I found out everything about the organisation, job and type of person required, by visiting the factory and talking to the staff there – including my interviewer!'

HOW LONG DID YOU DO THAT JOB?

This sounds like a daft question to the ill-prepared and naive interviewee who assumes it is being asked either because the interviewer is (still) trying to help him or her relax, or as a result of a mislaid application form or curriculum vitae. It is not ridiculous, nor is it raised for these reasons. You may hear it if you have held a job for a very short or an extremely long period of time – and the interviewer wishes to know why. Perhaps you lose interest quickly and want to move, which may not be what the interviewer is looking for in an employee. Alternatively, you might be happy to stay in the same post year after year, whereas your interviewer is seeking someone with more ambition and drive. Give a straight answer, such as 'Four months, from April

78

to August' or 'Twelve years, from June 1980 to July 1992'. Then wait for the follow-up.

WHY DID YOU HOLD THAT JOB FOR SUCH A SHORT TIME?

A crunch question, and one which needs to be answered carefully if you are to stay in contention for this job. All sorts of negative thoughts may be spinning around in the interviewer's mind. He or she may be wondering whether you were incapable of doing the job and quit, if you were sacked because you were a troublemaker or whether you walked out to do something else, which might perhaps involve easier work. Hopefully, your interviewer is trying to retain an open mind but these nagging doubts and worries are hardly surprising if he or she knows your last job lasted for only a few short weeks or months. You need to quash these thoughts – hard and fast.

It may be that this was a temporary post and you should explain this, backing up your comments by inviting your interviewer to approach the employer for a reference, to prove that he or she thinks highly of you. As an example, 'Well it was a temporary job, really. McGraws needed someone to fill in for a few months whilst one of the team was away on maternity leave, and I fitted the bill. We were both very happy with the arrangement, although I felt rather sad when I eventually left. Mr Munglani, my boss, said he'd be delighted to give me a reference so I've put the details on the back of the application form, should you wish to approach him for reference purposes.'

If this was a permanent job which ended abruptly, then it is wise to admit the reasons. Most likely, you were unsuited to the post, and both you *and* the organisation made a mistake. Hopefully, you left on good terms, and the employer will not speak badly of you if contacted. Ideally, you would say something like this: 'To be honest, the job and I weren't well matched. It wasn't what I thought it was – I didn't have the responsibilities I expected to have. I talked it over with my boss and we agreed it would be best if we parted ways. I stayed on until a successor was found, then we shook hands and I left.' You sound fair, honest and a decent person – just what *this* interviewer wants.

WHY HAVE YOU HAD SO MANY JOBS?

A tough question developing from the last one, and asked for the same purpose – to confirm or remove the suspicion that you cannot hold down a job, whatever the cause. One mistake will almost certainly be overlooked if you have explained it carefully, and in a balanced and reasonable manner. Two, three, four or more is not so easy. Perhaps you have had genuine and understandable reasons for changing employment so often – your parents moved home frequently and you went with them in your teenage years, you were made redundant because of the recession, a firm ceased trading, and so forth. Possibly you were transferred or promoted! If so, work through each job, explaining the situation in a concise manner.

'Various reasons. After leaving school, I went to work at Lukin's on the Copdock Industrial Estate but was made redundant after eight months because they needed to reduce their workforce by twenty per cent. They operated a first in, last out policy there. Then I went to Smithsons in Carr Street but that closed down after I had been there for a year and had just been promoted. I was at Thompson and Sons in Ferringham for four years, and had three jobs there, being transferred to another department once and being promoted to more senior positions on two occasions.' Bingo! You have managed to avert disaster by talking briefly about the different posts, and making sense of the changes.

If you have moved about because you were unable to settle into a job you liked, or have been dismissed from your employment, then it is sensible to be honest about it. Own up to your mistakes – you were too young and did not know what you wanted to do, you took on jobs for which you had insufficient experience and decided with the employer that it would be best for you to leave, and so on. Show that you have gained from your jobs, though, picking up skills, knowledge and experience along the way and – most important of all – indicate that you do know what you now wish to do, and have the talents and abilities to do it.

For example: 'I've had six or seven jobs over the past few years because I didn't really know what I wanted to do until now. I was drifting really, although I've acquired some useful skills in each post – I was taught to type at Hunters, I studied for my business and finance diploma on a day-release basis at Sanderson and Hebbs and worked on the checkouts at Kwids In, the supermarket, which got me used to dealing with the public and handling money. I realised I was going nowhere, though, and sat down with a careers adviser and discussed my options. I decided I wanted to join a bank or a building society as a clerk because of the work and job prospects – and as I've the skills needed to do this job well.'

WHY HAVE YOU HAD THAT JOB FOR SUCH A LONG TIME?

Another key question which needs to be answered successfully. The interviewer knows about your last job and your skills, knowledge and experiences but now wishes to find out more about you, the person. He or she is worried that you are either unambitious or unpromotable – neither of which are likely to inspire a job offer on this occasion. To remain on course, you must show that these shortcomings do not apply to you. Here is what you could say: 'Eight years sounds a long time but it's flown past. You see the company's forever expanding, locally, nationally and then internationally, so my job has changed continually and satisfied my personal ambitions. It's also felt as though I've been promoted a lot, because my department's expanded so often with new staff, then computerisation and various added responsibilities. I've kept the same job title – but I'm pleased my wages have gone up!'

WHY DID YOU LEAVE YOUR LAST JOB?

This is an inevitable question at an interview, and is raised for the same purpose as 'Why did you hold that job for such a short

DISCUSSING PREVIOUS EMPLOYMENT: AN ACTION CHECKLIST

Take some time to work out what you will say in reply to these questions. Sketch out ideas for answers.

Tell me about your last job

What have you learned from that job?

What did you like about the job?

What did you think of your boss?

How did you get that job?

What did you dislike about the job

How long did you do that job?

What problems did you have to deal with?

How did you handle that task?

DISCUSSING PREVIOUS EMPLOYMENT: AN ACTION CHECKLIST

Why did you hold that job for such a short time?

Why have you had so many jobs?

Why have you had that job for such a long time?

Why did you leave your last job?

time?' and 'Why have you had so many jobs?' Again, you need to show that you left for a good reason *and* with the employer's goodwill, substantiated with a promise of a decent reference. 'I'd gone as far as I could go at Roebucks – there were no real oppor- tunties for promotion because it was a small concern. I talked things through with Mrs Roebuck and we decided I should look around for a new job, staying on there until I had found one. Mrs Roebuck will give me a good reference, on request.'

If you were sacked, admit it. There is little point in trying to cover this up, because the interviewer is going to want to approach your former employer for a reference before taking you on. Hopefully, you can say something along the lines of: 'To be frank, my contract wasn't renewed at the end of my three-month probation period. The personnel manager and I talked together after a couple of months and decided I should leave on amicable terms. She wanted me to switch into the accounts department, whereas I wished to progress in sales. We'd reached a stalemate so we called it a day.' Fair enough – and a good enough reason not to lose you this job.

VIEWING THIS VACANCY

Now that your previous employment has been covered in the most complete and thorough manner, your interviewer should progress towards the job you have applied for. Whatever your age or experience, a number of questions will be put to you, and will have to be answered successfully if you are to go on to be a winner. These are some of the questions that are most likely to be asked:

- Tell me about this job
- What part of the job most appeals to you?
- What part of the job least appeals to you?
- What qualities are needed to do this job well?
- What makes you think you can do this job?

– How much money do you want?

TELL ME ABOUT THIS JOB

Here, the interviewer wishes to know whether you really want the job, and have therefore made the effort to find out all about it. He or she also needs to be sure that you have a realistic image of it, recognising its positive *and* negative aspects. There is little point in recruiting someone who is unaware of the shortcomings of the job, and who might resign when these become apparent. This is an easy-to-answer question if – and only if – you have done your homework, by studying the advertisement, obtaining a job description, talking to the outgoing employee, and so on. Describe it briefly, making a point of commenting on its best and worst features. Remember not to be irrelevant, and avoid talking too much.

'The job is as an assistant in the admin office here, which has a staff of ten, and is run by Mrs Yip, the office manager. It involves doing a bit of everything – sort out the post, photocopying incoming and outgoing mail, filing, typing correspondence, maintaining stationery supplies, keeping the office tidy, running errands and making tea and coffee. It's a nine-to-five job, offering £6,500 per year, no overtime, eighteen days' holiday each year and staff discounts of ten per cent on the company's goods. There's a friendly atmosphere and a good working environment on the site.' Clearly, you know what's what, and can elaborate if pressed further.

WHAT PART OF THE JOB MOST APPEALS TO YOU?

The obvious follow up to 'Tell me about this job', this question could also be phrased as 'What interests you most about this job?', 'What do you like about this job?' and 'What are you looking forward to doing in this job?' It is asked for the same reasons as 'Tell me about this job' and ought to be answered along similar lines. 'Well, I'll be a Jack – or Jacquie! – of all trades, and I think that's what appeals to me most of all. It'll give me the chance to learn the ins and outs of office life, who does what, how it runs, how it helps and liaises with other departments, and so on. I realise I'm starting at the bottom as everyone has to do and that it'll be hard work – I guess I'll be a dogsbody really – but it's a great opportunity to join Bonetti's and get my first step on to the ladder.' Whatever you say, stay down to earth.

WHAT PART OF THE JOB LEAST APPEALS TO YOU?

'What interests you least about this job?', 'What do you dislike about this job?', 'What are you not looking forward to doing in this job?' – however the question is raised, show that you are fully familiar with the drawbacks of the work, accept them *and* are still enthusiastic about the job. For example, you could say this: 'The job has some mundane tasks that need doing day in and day out – sorting, filing photocopying, stamping, franking and the like – but that's all part of the job, isn't it? I'm well aware of the less exciting aspects of the work but they're all necessary and will help me learn about office life. No matter what I do, I always tackle every task with equal enthusiasm, and do it to the best of my ability. My form tutor, Mr Jones, will confirm that.'

WHAT QUALITIES ARE NEEDED TO DO THIS JOB WELL?

With this question, the interviewer is digging in to see how far you have researched and thought carefully about the job. He or she knows that you are well aware of the various tasks, duties, pluses and minuses of the job, but now wants to find out whether you have learned of or calculated what attributes you should have to be able to do it well. What a brilliant opportunity this is for you to really impress your interviewer – assuming that you did all that vital preliminary work. Contemplating the employee specification, pick out and refer to some of the essential and desirable requirements, in a brief and concise manner.

'To be a telephonist in a customer relations department, I think you need various qualities. You must be a good listener – friendly and sympathetic. You need to be able to speak clearly, without a speech impediment. It's very important to have a full knowledge of the firm, its goods and services, and its policies with regard to customer complaints, and returns. You have to know what you can and cannot do for customers, and when you should refer a matter to a supervisor.' This is a quality answer, which invites a follow-on question about you.

WHAT MAKES YOU THINK YOU CAN DO THIS JOB?

A very popular question, also phrased as 'Why should we employ you?' and 'What makes you the right person for this job?', and an open invitation for you to state your qualities so that the interviewer can compare them with those in the employee specification. Your answer is obvious – and unbeatable! You are fully familiar with the varied attributes that the interviewer is seeking and are conscious of your strengths, from that initial self-assessment. Match them up, refer to them in turn, and substantiate your words with supporting evidence, as and where possible. Do not talk too much, though, as this may bore the interviewer.

'Well, I believe I have all the key qualities required to be a telephonist. I speak clearly and can hold a conversation as we are doing now. I know all about the firm – you'll recall I told you what I'd found out at the beginning of the interview when you said "Shall I talk about the organisation?" I've also learned about your policies towards customer complaints and returns. You issue every telephonist with a ten-point checklist of do's and don'ts when talking to customers. And here it is . . .'

HOW MUCH MONEY DO YOU WANT?

A tricky question, and one which can be difficult to answer successfully. The interviewer invariably has a minimum and maximum figure in mind and wants to be sure that your salary will fall within these limits. Go below this range, and you sound unambitious, and could even find yourself working for a salary which is less than the firm originally intended to offer. Go too high and you appear greedy, and might be immediately discounted for the job because your demands are viewed as unrealistic. Hopefully, the job advertisement stated a specific figure or a range of figures, or you have found out the likely salary from your research. Thus, you can reply, 'The advertisement quotes £9,000 per year, which is fine for me' or 'I understand you're looking between £8,000 and £10,000 and I hope you'll make me an offer within that range.' Add a comment like this: 'At the moment I'm more concerned with getting this job than the money, as it's what I've always wanted to do.'

CONTEMPLATING FUTURE EMPLOYMENT

Next, the conversation will move naturally on to how you see yourself progressing within the job market in the coming months and years. In all probability, your interviewer will not spend much time focusing on this topic, as the further ahead you look, the less relevant it becomes to the present situation. Nevertheless, there are a few, choice questions which will almost certainly be asked because the answers will help the interviewer to reach a decision about you. Expect to have to respond to these ones:

- Are you pursuing other jobs?
- What will you do if you fail to get this job?
- If offered this job, how long would you stay with us?
- Where do you see yourself in five years?

ARE YOU PURSUING OTHER JOBS?

A tough one! This – and the rather more specific 'Are you considering any other offers at the moment?' – needs to be handled with tact. Obviously, the interviewer realises that you are looking at other vacancies, but hopes that this one is at the top of your list. He or she does not wish to recruit a half-hearted person who only takes up the offer because nothing else is available, and who might subsequently resign suddenly if another, better

89

VIEWING THIS VACANCY: AN ACTION CHECKLIST

Note the key points you need to make in response to questions about the job you have applied for. Be ready with loose and flexible answers, however the questions are phrased.

Tell me about this job

What qualities are needed to do this job well?

What part of the job most appeals to you?

What makes you think you can do this job?

What part of the job least appeals to you?

How much money do you want?

offer is made. Hence, it is wise to state that you are not actively pursuing other jobs because this is very much your first choice, but there are other possibilities in the pipeline. It can do no harm to indicate that alternative jobs exist, so long as you do not hammer the point home. It may nudge the interviewer in the right direction.

Here is what you might say: 'No, I want this job more than anything else because I really believe I've got the skills, knowledge and experience to do it. I'm aware that other jobs are available in this field but I hope that I don't need to go after them. This is the job I'm concentrating on – it's the one that I want.' If you are asked about receiving other offers, then your answer must be a resounding 'No!' Your interviewer will not be convinced that this is the job you want if you have gone so far with another application, nor will he or she let you play one offer against another, and so on. Say 'Yes' and you are finished on this occasion.

WHAT WILL YOU DO IF YOU FAIL TO GET THIS JOB?
A natural follow-up to 'Are you pursuing other jobs?' to see how committed you are to getting this job. Shoot back an answer which shows that commitment *and* stresses your suitability for the post. For example, 'Well, I really hope I don't fail because I'm sure I'm the right person for this job. I've the qualifications you want, I've done a very similar job for three years, and I'm an industrious and conscientious worker, as my last employer will confirm. I'm not thinking about what will happen if I don't succeed because I'm determined to win this job.' Avoid going over the top, though. Comments like 'I'm not going to fail' or even 'I never fail' will just alienate the interviewer, who *will* fail you straight away.

If you are pressed further about your likely activities following a possible rejection for this position, then it is a good idea to respond along similar lines, highlighting how much you want the job, and how well matched you are to it. 'If you turned me down, I'd be extremely disappointed because I know that the job

92

and I are right for each other in so many ways . . . Still . . . I guess I'd then have to look for a comparable post which was suited to my skills, knowledge and experience, and in an expanding firm like yours which offers me lots of chances to get ahead.'

IF OFFERED THIS JOB, HOW LONG WOULD YOU STAY WITH US?

This is a more positive question from your interviewer but one which is asked for the same reasons as 'What will you do if you fail to get this job?' Once more, he or she is trying to discover how much you wish to have this job, and whether it is a stopgap until something else comes along or is a significant part of your career plan. Tell the interviewer what he or she wants to hear – 'I hope to stay with you on a long-term basis. The job and I are ideally suited, and the work is fulfilling. The company and I are equally ambitious, and you offer me plenty of opportunities to progress if I do well. I can't think of any reason why I'd want to leave.' Spot-on – a winning answer to a tricky question!

WHERE DO YOU SEE YOURSELF IN FIVE YEARS?

A very popular question raised by the interviewer in another attempt to assess your desire to win this job and to work for the organisation on a permanent, lengthy basis. He or she probably wants to hear that you are ambitious and keen to get ahead but almost invariably wishes this to be within the firm. Your interviewer will be offended if you indicate that you will have to leave to become more successful, nor will he or she want to spend time and money training you, if you are planning to depart at some stage. Thus, 'I see myself working here, moving up through the organisation as I learn the ropes and other vacancies arise for which I am suited. I'm keen to be successful and feel sure I can succeed in your firm. It's where I want to be.'

CONTEMPLATING FUTURE EMPLOYMENT: AN ACTION CHECKLIST

Consider the following questions carefully, one at a time. Then list the major points to be raised during the questioning about your forthcoming plans.

Are you pursuing other jobs?

What will you do if you fail to get this job?

If offered this job, how long would you stay with us?

Where do you see yourself in five years?

5 PERSONALITY MATTERS

Probing your Personality
Looking at Leisure Activities
Invading your Privacy

5 PERSONALITY MATTERS

Now that your past, present and future employment has been covered in some detail, your interviewer will want to press on to find out more about you as a person. He or she will wish to probe your personality, look at your leisure activities and might go so far as to invade your privacy, by asking personal and even offensive questions about your private life. You need to be well prepared for these questions and be ready to give the right answers – assuming that you still want this job!

PROBING YOUR PERSONALITY

Whoever you are, do expect to be asked about your personality, and how you see yourself as a person. This is a good opportunity for you to build upon the successful answers given to earlier questions about your employment, and to convince the interviewer that you are ideal for the job. These are some of the most common questions you might face:

- What are you like as a person?
- What are your likes?
- What are your dislikes?
- What are your strengths?
- What are your weaknesses?
- Do you prefer working with others or on your own?

WHAT ARE YOU LIKE AS A PERSON?

This question is asked because the interviewer wants to hear you describe yourself, to assess how far your personal qualities match the ones that were written down on the employee specification. As important, he or she wishes to listen to you talk about yourself, to check if it is in an arrogant or modest manner, and so on. The way in which you talk will tell him or her as much about you as what you say. From your research into the type of person required and your self-assessment, you should know exactly how to reply, referring to the essential and desirable requirements that you fulfil, and substantiating your comments as far as possible. Stay calm as you speak – and do not show off!

You might say something like this: 'I think I'm a friendly sort of person. I seem to mix well with all types of people. In my last job, my boss received several letters from customers telling him how much they appreciated my pleasant and helpful service. And they weren't from my mum! I'm hard-working too. I'll stick at a task until it's done, whether that means staying on in the office into the evenings, or working at home at the weekends. My referees will confirm that in their references. I like to think I'm ambitious as well. I give all I've got to the work I'm doing but I'm keen to progress to new challenges as they arise. That's why I want this job!'

WHAT ARE YOUR LIKES?

A rather vague question used instead of or in addition to 'What are you like as a person?', and asked for the same basic reasons. Your interviewer wants to know what you will say and how you will say it. Again, your response should be similar to the last one. For example: 'I like challenges. I always set personal goals to try to push myself that bit further and to feel I've achieved something. For example, when I was at Camplins we were each expected to produce fifty units per day. I aimed for sixty, and averaged fifty-seven, which kept my boss happy, gave me a useful bonus and still made me work harder to beat that goal. I did it too, in my last week there.' Whatever you say, stay relevant by linking your qualities to the job – your love of Chinese take-aways, 1950s movies and Scunthorpe United Football Club will not interest the interviewer in the least.

WHAT ARE YOUR DISLIKES?

This is the inevitable follow-up to 'What are your likes?' as your interviewer seeks to dig out a little more detail about you, to see how compatible you really are for this post. You need to be very careful here – it is easy to talk yourself out of a job offer over what appears to be a simple and innocuous question. Talk about your dislikes with regard to your work, whilst being especially wary of criticising your former boss or colleagues, or implying that you are unhappy about working hard, doing boring tasks or dealing with the less pleasant aspects of your work. Also, steer clear of launching into a tirade about your dislike of pot noodles, television soaps, synchronised swimming and other trivia. Your interviewer does not want to know about these at all.

Here is what you could say in response to this question, cleverly turning it to your advantage to promote your qualities again: 'I suppose I dislike failure. It bothers me if I can't master a task or achieve a goal. I remember when I worked in the accounts office at Cohens in the High Road and they computerised all of their books and records. I just couldn't get the hang of the new system to start with, and it really troubled me. I stuck with it, though, reading the manual, and I even went on a course at the local college before I cracked the system. It took me time to get there, but now I can use computers with ease. I was teaching new recruits how to use them before I left.'

WHAT ARE YOUR STRENGTHS?

This is it! The question you have probably been waiting for has arisen. Your interviewer wishes to know about your good points to see if they tally with the statements on that employee specification, and you are ready to respond by reeling off the list of strengths you wrote down when you were assessing yourself. Go for it, but do be brief and selective. Avoid droning on and on and on, mentioning everything under the sun. Back up your words with examples, and proof whenever you can. Stay cool and modest too – it is so easy to sound like a braggart when replying to this key question.

'That's a tough one! . . . I think I've got various personal qualities which I'll bring to the job of a media sales executive. I'm a good communicator. I speak clearly. I explain complex matters in a concise manner. For example, "ears", "solus positions" and "island positions" mean nothing to most clients, so let's explain that respectively they're the spaces to the sides of the front-page title, the only adverts on a page, and advertisements surrounded by editorial text. I'm friendly, too, and try to get on with everyone from sole traders to managing directors. In my last job for Razz FM radio, I'd be talking to a small shopkeeper in the morning and meeting the managing director of a public limited company in the afternoon.'

WHAT ARE YOUR WEAKNESSES?

Here, your interviewer is trying to uncover your hidden side, asking you to tell him or her about your shortcomings. You are being invited to lose that job! Instead, you are going to win it, by switching from weaknesses to strengths, like this: 'I think I'm very demanding. I expect a lot from myself. I believe that if you want to succeed you have to get up and do it for yourself. That's what I do and why I always accept a low basic salary with a higher commission in a new job. I've confidence in myself and am sure I'll earn my money.' Spot-on – within a few, short sentences you've moved from a negative to a positive impression. The interviewer will be won over.

DO YOU PREFER WORKING WITH OTHERS OR ON YOUR OWN?

Up until now, the interviewer has probed your personality by asking you broad questions about yourself, and has listened to your replies to compare and contrast you with the type of person needed to do the job. Naturally, there will be one or two essential or desirable requirements which have not been covered by your conversation, so more direct questions will then be asked – 'Do you like working in a team?', 'Do you like working alone?' or 'Do you prefer working with others or on your own?' If you have done your research, you will know whether the job involves solitary or team work, and can thus give the 'right' answer. Do not be too definite though – remember the job could change or lead on to other work which requires different qualities.

This is what you might say: 'Well, I like to think that I'm a team person who gets on well with people around me, and makes a significant contribution to the workload. My previous jobs have all involved fitting into a group, and my employers have complimented me on my ability to do this successfully, as I'm sure they'll confirm in my references. However, I can also work well on my own, setting my own goals and deadlines, and achieving them. If the need arose in this job, I certainly wouldn't let anyone down.' A good response – you have managed to sound positive whilst hedging your bets. A tricky task!

Of course, many other questions like this could be asked about the various requirements which have not been discussed so far. These might include 'Do you like regular or irregular hours?', 'Do you have initiative?', 'Can you take orders?', 'Can you work to a deadline?' and 'Are you willing to move about?' All of these questions sound different but are very similar to 'Do you prefer working with others or on your own?', and need to be answered in the same way. You should know what the reply ought to be, and must attempt to back up your response with substantiating comments.

Taking 'Can you work to a deadline?' as an example, you could say 'Yes, definitely. In my last job, I was responsible for producing weekly sales reports for my department head from returns submitted by agents in the field. I was always working against the clock, chasing agents, collecting and interpreting the material, noting it down in a concise and readable manner, and

PROBING YOUR PERSONALITY: AN ACTION CHECKLIST

Work out what you might say in reply to questions about your personality, and jot down the points you wish to cover.

What are you like as a person?

What are your strengths?

What are your likes?

What are your weaknesses?

What are your dislikes?

Do you prefer working with others or on your own?

submitting it at the right time. I didn't miss a deadline in six years – nearly three hundred reports went in on time.' If that is what is required in this post, it sounds as though you will get it, and deservedly so.

LOOKING AT LEISURE ACTIVITIES

With a better knowledge of your personality, the interviewer is likely to try to add to his or her understanding of you as a person by finding out what you do in your free time. Here are some popular questions asked about this topic:

– What do you do in the evenings and at weekends?
– Tell me about your hobbies
– Do you belong to any clubs or societies?
– Do you like sports?
– What books do you read?
– Which newspaper do you read?
– What did you read about in this morning's edition?
– Do you have any money-making schemes on the go?

WHAT DO YOU DO IN THE EVENINGS AND AT WEEKENDS?

This is a good question which your interviewer hopes will draw you into discussing what you do out of hours, in turn revealing more about yourself. Perhaps you take work home with you from time to time, which might be regarded as a sign of a dedicated, hard-working employee. Possibly, you participate in various activities – running a scout troop, laying a patio, painting landscapes and so on – which indicate that you have attributes that are well suited to this job, whether leadership, manual or artistic skills, and so forth. Whatever you do and choose to refer to, make sure it involves doing something constructive and worthwhile, and is job-related if possible. Slumping in front of the television and snoring the evening away will not impress anyone.

This is what you might say: 'It depends, really. I commuted in my last job and didn't get home until seven . . . half past seven sometimes. By the time we'd eaten and washed up, there wasn't much time left to do very much. I'm a keen DIY enthusiast, though, and in the odd evening and at most weekends over the past year I've been planning and then building an extension to the back of the house. It'll give us a small study to work in – my wife runs a typing and proofreading service from home, and I can use it at the weekends if I bring any work back with me. I can shut myself away from the children, and do it in peace!'

TELL ME ABOUT YOUR HOBBIES

This may be asked instead of 'What do you do in the evenings and at weekends?' It is a broader question, raised for the same purpose and likely to produce a similar response because your hobbies will probably be carried out in the evenings and at weekends. As often, it will follow the opening question and be phrased as 'Tell me about your scout troop', 'Tell me about laying a patio', 'Tell me about your watercolours' or 'Tell me about your DIY work'. Your interviewer is pushing to discover precisely what you do, how long you have done it for, why you do it and so on. He or she wants to complete the picture of you – and ensure that this really is your hobby and not something you are mentioning to appear impressive. It is surprising how many interviewees develop an interest in helping the sick and the elderly around the time of their interview.

Build upon your previous reply, using language which is simple to understand. Too technical, and your interviewer will be confused. Too simplistic, though, and he or she may feel patronised. Keep your comments brief and to the point. It is easy to become carried away in the excitement of finding a fellow enthusiast – but remember the interviewer is interested in you, *not* the hobby itself. 'I've always been keen on DIY since I was a boy. My dad was a builder and I learned a great deal from him. I've added a lot to all of the houses we've lived in, starting with shelves and progressing to central-heating systems and loft conversions. This extension is my most ambitious project yet and will be of enormous benefit to all of us when it's finished.'

DO YOU BELONG TO ANY CLUBS OR SOCIETIES?

A more direct question which crops up when interviewees mention 'clubbable' hobbies without referring to clubs or societies. As a general rule, interviewers like to see interviewees belonging to such organisations as it indicates that they are team members who will fit in, and mix well with fellow employees. If you do belong to a club or society, say so: 'Yes, I'm a member of the Rustlingleigh Bowls Club. We meet on Sunday mornings to play against each other and then take on other club sides once or twice a month on Monday evenings. It's great fun. There's a smashing camaraderie there.' If not, state that you would like to: 'Unfortunately not. Even though creative writing is a fairly solitary craft, I'd like to join a writers' circle but there isn't one locally. I'm thinking of setting one up – I'm sure it would be enjoyable and informative to exchange ideas.' A team person – and showing initiative too!

DO YOU LIKE SPORTS?

Another direct question raised by interviewers who want their employees to participate in sporting activities so that they stay fit and healthy, and preferably in group sports so they are seen to be team members. If you play sport, explain what you do: 'Yes, I'm keen on tennis and play most Sundays up at Sandby Park. I'm not very good at the moment because I've only started playing again after having my children, but I hope to represent the team in the local championships next year.' If you do not participate, you still need to stress how healthy you are: 'Yes, I take my sons to football, cricket and all the usual things but I don't play myself. Bit past it nowadays! I keep in shape, though – I don't smoke, my weight's the same as it was twenty years ago and I still do twenty press-ups every morning.'

WHAT BOOKS DO YOU READ?

What a question! Your interviewer is really digging deep to get to know you – take it as a compliment as he or she probably would not go so far unless you were close to an offer. Think carefully about your reply to decide what will show in a favourable light. Saying that you have recently been reading books about job hunting, the type of work you hope to do or the trade or industry you will be working in will suggest you are enthusiastic about this job, and are determined to win it. 'Lately I've been reading Jeanette Reynold's book *Nursery Retailing: Towards 2000*, published by Nursery Retailer Publications. It gave me a real insight into how smaller shops are fighting to survive against the out-of-town multiples and the ways in which the industry is going to develop in the coming years.'

Expect to be pressed further about your reading material, since many interviewees claim to read certain books simply to make themselves sound clever and informed. 'What did you think of that book?', 'Which bits did you like best?', 'Which parts were most informative?' and so on may be asked – so make sure you really have studied the book and can answer the question correctly. 'Overall, I thought it was a very revealing text. The most relevant parts were the appendices, surprisingly enough. These consisted of case studies made up of interviews with small nursery traders who had either been forced out of business by the big concerns or who were struggling to compete in terms of location, stock range, price and so on. Some of the stories were very moving.'

Your interviewer might also press you about the books which you read for pleasure, believing that these will tell him or her more about you. Think about the types of books that the ideal employee might read, which hopefully will be what you look at too. If in doubt, stick to the non-offensive middle ground – Jeffrey Archer, Ruth Rendell, Jilly Cooper – so long as you are able to comment on his or her latest title if questioned further. Avoid quoting *The Complete Works of Shakespeare* or similar titles which will make you sound pretentious, or anything too bloodthirsty.

A penchant for stomach–churning books is unlikely to show you in a favourable light.

WHICH NEWSPAPER DO YOU READ?

Another popular question, much the same as 'What books do you read?' and asked for the same reason – to get to know you better. Many interviewers believe they can learn much about an interviewee from the newspaper he or she reads, and they may be correct. As an example, the *Sun* or another tabloid may be read by a prospective mechanic but is likely to be considered less appropriate reading material for a would-be college lecturer, who might be expected to study *The Guardian* or another broadsheet. You will probably read what the ideal employee looks at, and can give an appropriate response: 'I read *The Independent*. It deals with important stories instead of salacious or trivial ones. It sees both viewpoints too, which I like. Some papers are too biased for my tastes.'

WHAT DID YOU READ ABOUT IN THIS MORNING'S EDITION?

This is a rogue question which pops up surprisingly often, as a follow-on to 'Which newspaper do you read?' The interviewer may be asking it to see if you really do study the newspaper you claim to read – perhaps you are a closet *Daily Sport* reader instead! More likely, he or she wants to know what caught your eye, and interested you, simply to learn more about you as a person, and your interests. It might even be raised because there was something in the newspapers this morning about the firm, one of its competitors or the industry, and your interviewer believes you should have read it if you really want the job.

A good, play-safe answer that will avoid any potential embarrassment is this: 'To be honest, I haven't yet had a chance to look at today's paper. I've been concentrating on preparing for this interview – rereading the job advertisement, checking over my curriculum vitae and studying your company's literature. I can't tell you what's in the *Financial Times* but I know your latest company report inside out!' Hopefully, the interviewer will ask you to comment further and you can tell him or her a little more about what you have read – and win that job!

If a feature about the organisation, its rivals or the industry was in the morning newspaper, you may prefer to refer to it, to show you are up to date with the latest information, and are enthusiastic about the job. 'I read about your plans to build a new plant over at Benham in order to increase production to meet demand from your overseas customers in Scandinavia. You'd be looking to recruit three hundred people over the next eighteen months – I hope I'm one of them!' This is a competent reply. It should go down well.

DO YOU HAVE ANY MONEY-MAKING SCHEMES ON THE GO?

Be careful! This is a devilish question, and a difficult one to answer. Say 'No' and you appear to have no initiative at all. Reply with a 'Yes' and the interviewer may be concerned that they will affect your work. You are damned if you do, and damned if you do not. It may be wise to hedge your bets if you can. 'No. There are various things that I do out of work, such as that sponsored walk I mentioned, but I've no moonlighting jobs to earn extra money! I concentrate on the nine-to-five job. That's more important.' Alternatively, 'Yes, I've sold some of my paintings now and then through local galleries, but it's just a part-time hobby. It doesn't interfere with my work at all.' Whatever you say, play safe with this one.

INVADING YOUR PRIVACY

Now considering you seriously for the job, your interviewer might ask you questions about your private life in an effort to further his or her understanding of you. On occasions, some of these questions may be relevant but more often are not. Inevitably, they can be embarrassing and even unpleasant for you to

LOOKING AT LEISURE ACTIVITIES: AN ACTION CHECKLIST

Do prepare well for questions about what you do in your free time, by making a note of what you want to talk about.

What do you do in the evenings and at weekends?

What books do you read?

Tell me about your hobbies

Which newspaper do you read?

Do you belong to any clubs or societies?

What did you read about in this morning's edition?

Do you like sports?

Do you have any money-making schemes on the go?

answer, yet they can be surprisingly helpful in one respect – you may reach the conclusion that you do not want to work for a person who asks unnecessary and intrusive questions. He or she could be an ogre of a boss and it is better to find this out now, instead of later on when you are at work. If the interviewer covers this topic – and many will not because they realise it is usually inappropriate – the following questions may arise:

- Are you married?
- What does your partner do?
- How does your partner feel about your application for this job?
- If your partner moves away, will you go too?
- Why are you unmarried?
- Do you have children?
- What will you do if your children are sick?
- Do you intend to have children?
- How do you get on with white people?

ARE YOU MARRIED?

Questions about your marital status may crop up in your interview. 'Are you married?' and 'Are you planning to marry?' could be acceptable in some circumstances, such as when a brewery is hoping to recruit a married couple to run a pub, and the information was not included on a submitted curriculum vitae. Clearly, these are easy to answer: 'Yes, I'm married to Yvonne. We've been together for ten years' or 'Yes, I'm going to marry my fiancé Paul in the autumn.' If you are unmarried and have no plans to marry in the immediate future, or are divorced, say 'No', and wait for the follow-on questions.

WHAT DOES YOUR PARTNER DO?

This may be regarded as a fair question in some instances. For example, if you want to be installed as the manager of an off-licence, newsagent or another, similar business, your partner may be expected to help you in some capacity, which is unlikely to be possible if he or she is pursuing a rewarding career elsewhere. Alternatively, your partner might work in the same trade or industry which could be considered an advantage, or as a disadvantage if he or she is employed by a rival concern. By and large, this is probably not an unreasonable question to put to you. Do not take offence.

You will know from your research if the question is a valid one, and mindful of that job description and employee specification can give a winning response to promote yourself. As an example, you could say something like: 'Fortunately, my husband, Clive, is in catering. He has his own business, and very useful it is too, when I've had clients round for dinner. He cooks the meal, and I win the accounts!' If the question seems irrelevant, reserve judgment on the direction that the interviewer is taking and provide a straightforward reply: 'Janet's in marketing. She's an assistant at Phoenix Construction, the building firm over in Midchester Park.' Then see what questions come next.

HOW DOES YOUR PARTNER FEEL ABOUT YOUR APPLICATION FOR THIS JOB?

The natural follow-up to 'What does your partner do?' and asked to see how supportive he or she is, perhaps to find out whether he or she will assist you in that off-licence, will wine and dine clients with you, or whatever. Your answer is obvious if you wish to receive a job offer – it should be very positive and backed up with a fitting example. 'She's very encouraging. We've always been extremely supportive of each other in our respective careers, and in all sorts of ways. For example, if one of us brings work home in the evenings, the other will feed and bath the children, and put them to bed.' Give a similar response even if the question appears less relevant to the job – and await developments.

IF YOUR PARTNER MOVES AWAY, WILL YOU GO TOO?

With this particular question, your interviewer is concerned that your partner's work takes priority over your employment, and you will hand in your notice if he or she is transferred or promoted to another job some distance away. The interviewer will then have to recruit someone else. To get that offer, you need to show how committed you are to winning *and* keeping this job on a long-term basis. You might say 'Of course, my partner may get a new job and we might move home, but that doesn't mean I'll pack my job in – far from it. I really want this job very much indeed, and I intend to hold on to it.' Reply in the same way if the question seems inappropriate – and start drawing conclusions about this interviewer.

WHY ARE YOU UNMARRIED?

'Why are you unmarried?', 'Why are you divorced?' and other similar questions about the reasons for your marital status appear to be unnecessary and insulting. They are too personal and should not be asked. The interviewer has gone too far in his or her attempts to find out more about you. 'I've never met the right person' or 'It didn't work out' may be appropriate responses – you are cool, polite but absolutely to the point to avoid encouraging this line of questioning. Hopefully, your interviewer will have the good sense to move on, away from this delicate personal subject.

Of course, you can say something along the lines of 'What's that got to do with anything?', 'Mind your own business', or even get up and walk out of that interview room there and then. It is best to stay put, though, and in control. It is in your interests to do so. You will increase your experience of interviews, interviewers and the types of questions that are asked, which will stand you in good stead next time. Hopefully, you might win a job offer as well, giving you the option to turn it down should you wish to do so. If you are going to tell the interviewer to stick the job, at least do it when it will hurt.

DO YOU HAVE CHILDREN?

This may be a valid question in some instances, such as when you are applying to be a journalist on a parenting magazine. Being a parent would be a distinct advantage to you when writing your articles. If this question is relevant in your situation, then your answer is obvious. You say either 'Yes' or 'No' – in which case you must try to indicate why being childless is *not* a disadvantage. 'Yes, I've two children. Jamie's five and Cara's one – just the age range you cover in *Mama*.' Alternatively, 'No, but I've worked with children for many years as a playgroup leader, and I'm an aunt to four boys and three girls, so I do know a lot about children.' If the question seems less relevant, give a similar reply which is polite, but discourages further conversation on the topic. Then wait for the inevitable following question.

WHAT WILL YOU DO IF YOUR CHILDREN ARE SICK?

Here, the interviewer is obviously thinking of making a job offer, but is worried that you will be unreliable because you are a parent. Not surprisingly, you will feel offended by this question. You would not be sitting here unless you felt confident about being a working parent, and could make arrangements to cover such eventualities as taking and collecting children from school, sickness, holidays and so on. To satisfy the intrviewer, say something like 'I've been a working parent for five years now, and have made sure that if problems arise they are handled either by my parents or my partner. I wouldn't be applying for this job if I wasn't one hundred per cent convinced that I could do it properly, come what may. My last employer will confirm my reliability.' Bite your tongue if you feel insulted. Get the job offer first – then speak your mind, if you want to.

INVADING YOUR PRIVACY: AN ACTION CHECKLIST

Hopefully, these questions will not arise in your interview, but you need to know what you are going to say if they do – even if it is the bluntest two-word response.

Are you married?

Why are you unmarried?

What does your partner do?

Do you have children?

How does your partner feel about your application for this job?

What will you do if your children are sick?

If your partner moves away, will you go too?

Do you intend to have children?

How do you get on with white people?

DO YOU INTEND TO HAVE CHILDREN?

This or the alternative 'Do you plan to have more children?' is asked because your interviewer is concerned that you will leave suddenly to have a baby. He or she will have wasted time and money on training you, only to have to begin the recruitment process again. To stay in contention for the job, the most sensible reply is along the lines of 'No, I don't have any plans to have children in the forseeable future.' If you are a woman in your twenties or thirties, the interviewer should realise and accept that you may have children at some stage, but it is wise not to suggest that this will happen soon, or is even definite. Again, if you are upset by the question, you can give a sharp reply or even get up and go, but try to bide your time. Wait until you have the upper hand.

HOW DO YOU GET ON WITH WHITE PEOPLE?

This and other questions such as 'Could you work for a white boss?', 'Will you be able to fit into a white team?' and 'Are you capable of handling a white workforce?' are rude and offensive and have all been asked of interviewees on occasions. If – and it is becoming an increasingly big if – you wish to work for this interviewer, you must give a very positive reply, and substantiate it if you can. 'I get on very well indeed with everyone I work with, whether bosses, colleagues, juniors, or whoever – and customers too. My previous boss, Mr Scott, will confirm in my reference how well I mix with people.' You retain the option of walking out at this point, or later on, if the interviewer persists with this line of questioning, but consider if it is in your best interests before you do.

6 MISCELLANEOUS TOPICS

Putting you to the Test
Handling Offbeat Questions
Checking Key Facts

6 MISCELLANEOUS TOPICS

Whether the interviewer follows the popular education–employment–leisure route or prefers to take a different approach, various miscellaneous topics may crop up either individually at regular intervals or all together towards the end of the interview. Your interviewer will want to put you to the test by asking you questions to see how you would act in certain circumstances, and you need to know how to deal with these properly. To be successful, you must also be able to handle offbeat questions, and be aware of what to say when the interviewer is checking key facts. Do not underestimate the importance of these miscellaneous questions – your answers to them could make or break your application.

PUTTING YOU TO THE TEST

Many questions are likely to be raised by the interviewer in an effort to learn what you would do in varied hypothetical situations, usually job-related ones. These questions could arise in your interview:

- Tell me a story
- Sell this pen to me
- What would you say to an angry customer returning faulty goods?
- How would you approach a supplier who had delivered the wrong goods?
- What would you do if your boss was unavailable to help you?

– What would you do if no procedure existed to resolve a particular problem?
– How would you handle a disagreement with your boss?
– What would you do if you fell out with a colleague?

TELL ME A STORY

What a question! It is asked to see how quickly you think and respond to an unexpected and (almost) unanswerable question, which may be what you will have to do in this job, when faced with customers, or whoever. Do not hesitate or ask for help, and avoid stuttering and stumbling as you speak. Never reply with 'Once upon a time . . .' as some interviewees do, as this sounds as though you are being sarcastic, and mocking the interviewer. Hit back with a brief and concise story about you and your most recent job, highlighting your strengths and suitability for this post.

This may be an appropriate answer: 'Okay. When I joined Sullivans, I was immediately given responsibility for introducing a new work system for producing the goods. Each member of the team had to do a particular task in a set period of time to maintain output. The team said it couldn't be done but I was sure that it could be. I wanted to implement the system without creating difficulties, so I sat down and did every task myself within the specified times. That way, I proved my point and won their respect. They knew I wouldn't ask them to do anything I couldn't do myself. A leader needs the support of the team – and that's how I got it on that occasion.'

SELL THIS PEN TO ME

You are going to be asked this question if the job you have applied for involves promoting or selling products or services to the trade or the general public. Whether a pen, pencil, paperweight or another item in the interview room is referred to, your interviewer wants to see how well you handle a sales situation, and hear what you say. To sell any product or service to a customer, you have to attract attention, create interest, install desire and inspire action, so your reply should adhere to these four steps, one way or another.

Here is what you might say about the interviewer's pen. 'Sure . . . take a good look at this pen. Can you see three things that set it apart from the others on the market? Look closely. It's that much thicker, so we can get more ink into it! It's also a sealed unit, so no more leaks! What's the third thing? Ah well, that's the price – there's a special offer on at the moment. You can buy five hundred for just £24.95 including VAT – that's under five pence each. What a bargain. The offer ends today, though, but I can phone through your order now to ensure you'll qualify – and I'll guarantee delivery by Friday!'

WHAT WOULD YOU SAY TO AN ANGRY CUSTOMER RETURNING FAULTY GOODS?

You must expect to face questions about how you would handle difficult scenarios at work, and will have to answer them successfully if you are to get this job. Some of the questions are likely to concern customers – 'What would you say to an angry customer returning faulty goods?', 'What would you do if you saw a customer stealing?' and 'What would you do if a customer collapsed in front of you?' are popular ones that crop up time and again. The interviewer is hoping you will say that you would react in the way that the ideal employee would do, which probably means following company procedures and referring to your boss if in doubt or when the matter exceeds your responsibilities.

Thus, your reply to this question should be something like this: 'Well, the policy here at Regan's for trainee and junior sales staff is that we listen to the customer and then look at the item to see what the problem is. If it was purchased less than one month ago and there is obviously a manufacturing fault we apologise and offer a replacement or a full refund if they ask for this. If the item was bought over a month before or we're unsure of the cause of the fault, we ask the assistant manager, Miss Cooke, to take over. We're polite and attentive towards the customer at all times.'

HOW WOULD YOU APPROACH A SUPPLIER WHO HAD DELIVERED THE WRONG GOODS?

Similar to 'What would you say to an angry customer returning faulty goods?' and asked for the same purpose – to see whether you would deal with the difficulty in the way that the ideal employee would do. Therefore, your answer to this and to comparable questions such as 'How would you handle a supplier who had not delivered goods on time?' must be along the same lines. For example: 'First of all, I'd check the original order and compare it to the delivery note and the goods delivered so I knew what we wanted and what we'd got. I'd then telephone the supplier, speaking to the sales department and telling them about the problem. After that, I'd pass the documents to the head of my department who is responsible for sorting out the paperwork, and taking such matters from there.'

WHAT WOULD YOU DO IF YOUR BOSS WAS UNAVAILABLE TO HELP YOU?

This is the natural follow-on to 'What would you say to an angry customer returning faulty goods?', 'How would you approach a supplier which had delivered the wrong goods?' and their like. Clearly, the interviewer wants to hear that you will show your initiative as much as you can without breaching established company procedures for such situations. Your reply might be something such as: 'I'd do my best to handle the situation myself so far as company rules allow, and would refer to a senior colleague or the next person up the line for advice or authorisation if I felt I was going beyond my responsibilities.'

WHAT WOULD YOU DO IF NO PROCEDURE EXISTED TO RESOLVE A PARTICULAR PROBLEM?

This is the alternative question which might follow 'What would you say to an angry customer returning faulty goods?',

'How would you approach a supplier who had delivered the wrong goods?' and similar, testing questions. Here, the interviewer is again expecting you to indicate that you would show initiative but without exceeding your authority. You could say: 'I'd use my initiative and do whatever seemed right in the circumstances. Naturally, I'd make sure that my boss knew and approved of my actions before I did anything and would pass the matter on to him or her if this was more appropriate.'

HOW WOULD YOU HANDLE A DISAGREEMENT WITH YOUR BOSS?

A crafty question! Your interviewer is trying to find out if you can take instructions from a boss without causing problems. He or she really wants to hear that there will not be any disagreements with your boss, rather than how you will handle them. Here is what you should say: 'Mmm, I don't know. To tell the truth, I've never fallen out with any of my bosses and can't imagine that I ever will. I hope I'd be given the opportunity to show my qualities at work and to make a contribution to the team, but at the end of the day the boss is the boss – and I'd do as I was told!'

WHAT WOULD YOU DO IF YOU FELL OUT WITH A COLLEAGUE?

This is another cunning question from an interviewer who is seeking to recruit someone who is a team person and gets on well with people without disagreeing with them. An appropriate response to this particular question is: 'I'm not sure – I haven't had any problems with any of my colleagues before and hope I never will. I think that everyone in a team should do their best to work with each other and get on well together, otherwise no one is happy and nothing gets done. We all lose out!'

If you are pressed further about the possibility of having to work with a difficult colleague, you could add: 'Well, if that happened – and I don't believe it will occur here – I'd do my best to talk things through with him, see his side, explain my own

PUTTING YOU TO THE TEST: AN ACTION CHECKLIST

Take another look at these testing questions, and make a note of what you want to say in response to them.

What would you do if your boss was unavailable to help you?

Tell me a story

Sell this pen to me

What would you do if no procedure existed to resolve a particular problem?

What would you say to an angry customer returning faulty goods?

How would you handle a disagreement with your boss?

How would you approach a supplier who had delivered the wrong goods?

What would you do if you fell out with a colleague?

and hope that we could come to an amicable compromise – even if it meant we agreed to disagree! If we couldn't even do that, then I think we should go to our boss, outline the problem and see if he or she could suggest a solution.'

HANDLING OFFBEAT QUESTIONS

Some of the questions raised during an interview can be offbeat, to say the least. Here is a selection of the more unusual ones which will need to be handled carefully:

- Who is your favourite historical figure?
- Who or what has been the biggest influence on your life?
- What is the most embarrassing thing that has ever happened to you?
- What would you most like to do with your life?
- What have you heard about this organisation?
- What do you think of me as an interviewer?
- What would you say if I said you had performed badly today?
- How would you respond if I said you were unsuitable for this job?
- What do you think of the Government's handling of recent events?

WHO IS YOUR FAVOURITE HISTORICAL FIGURE?

A weird question, which might also be phrased as 'Which cartoon character do you like most of all?' or 'Which person do you most admire in the world?' It is asked because your interviewer believes that the figure named will tell him or her something about you. He or she will asume that you identify with that person's qualities and share or at least strive towards them. Name a well-known person and mention his or her attributes which should be similar to those on the employee specification – 'George Clarkson, the founder of this company. He was inventive, hard-working and ambitious – qualities we all need to succeed at our work.' Take this question seriously – laugh, and you will lose that offer.

WHO OR WHAT HAS BEEN THE BIGGEST INFLUENCE ON YOUR LIFE?

Surprisingly similar to 'Who is your favourite historical figure?' or whatever, this question is raised for much the same reasons. Answer it in the same way, keeping your comments linked to the job so far as you can. You could state: 'My uncle, Roger Gates. He showed me that you get out of a job what you put into it. He was the first to arrive at work and the last to leave. He worked hard, through tea breaks and lunch breaks and into the evenings and weekends if necessary. He joined Timpsons at sixteen and was running the company by the time he was thirty.'

WHAT IS THE MOST EMBARRASSING THING THAT HAS EVER HAPPENED TO YOU?

Not as daft a question as it sounds, because the interviewer is trying to find out how you cope with embarrassing situations – which may arise now and again in the job you have applied for. Pick a job–related incident that will not reflect too badly on you and explain how you handled it, thus turning a minor weakness into a strength. 'On my first day at Butterworths, I had to make a huge pot of tea for everyone. I was so nervous, especially as I had to find the kettle, fill it with water, look around for the tea and sugar, go out for the milk, wash and dry the mugs and so on. Anyway, I did it, took it into the office and poured it out before I realised I hadn't boiled the kettle. They all had cold tea! Everybody laughed, but funnily enough it broke the ice and helped me to settle in. They all knew who I was and were really friendly afterwards. It was the best thing I could have done!'

WHAT WOULD YOU MOST LIKE TO DO WITH YOUR LIFE?

A probing question designed to discover more about the 'real' you. Keep your response down to earth and tied to the job, drawing in those essential and desirable requirements which you fulfil. As an example: 'Well, I'm hard-working and ambitious so I'd hope to achieve whatever my abilities and drive will allow me to. So far as work is concerned, I'd be looking to progress regularly up through the company, taking on new tasks and responsibilities as I learn and grow.' Even if the question is more hypothetical, such as 'What would you do if you won a million pounds?', attempt to give a similar answer, talking about setting goals, achieving ambitions and so on. It should impress the interviewer.

WHAT HAVE YOU HEARD ABOUT THIS ORGANISATION?

This is a popular question which might equally be raised with regard to 'products and services', 'the job', 'the workplace', or whatever. The interviewer may be trying to pick up on any rumours currently circulating inthe marketplace, or could simply be fishing for a compliment, which is not unknown. Presumably, you have only heard positive comments about the organisation otherwise you would not be sitting here, so your answer should satisfy the interviewer, regardless of his or her motives. 'Good things. EBS has a reputation as a successful and dynamic firm, as well as being a decent and generous employer – just the organisation I want to work for.' Keep quiet if you have heard niggly little complaints, as these may upset the interviewer and make you appear to be a petty-minded gossip.

WHAT DO YOU THINK OF ME AS AN INTERVIEWER?

An awkward question to answer! Your interviewer may be looking for a realistic and accurate assessment from you, or praise to bolster his or her ego. Hopefully, you can do both: 'I believe you're a very good interviewer. You've dealt with the main topics in turn, have asked me some probing questions and let me answer them fully – I couldn't ask for more!' Even if you have a low opinion of your interviewer, it is probably wise to be tactful, saying something like 'I think I've learned a lot from you about how to handle an interview, raise topics and questions and deal with interviews. I'll know what to do if I'm ever on your side of the desk!' This is a quality answer – you have told the truth, *and* pleased your interviewer.

WHAT WOULD YOU SAY IF I SAID YOU HAD PERFORMED BADLY TODAY?

Do not panic if you hear this question – it is quite a common one, raised to see how you react and respond to criticism, which is likely to occur in the job from time to time. Say this, or something similar: 'I'd be disappointed, because I prepared thoroughly for the interview. For example, I came in, looked round and picked up the job description and employee specification. I've answered all of your questions carefully, talking about my education, employment, leisure interests and personality to show you my qualities for the job. We've had a good, flowing conversation and have discussed all of the main areas in detail. I would have said I'd performed well.' Whatever is stated, stay calm, steadily proving that the interviewer is wrong without offending him or her. As always, draw in your key strengths when possible.

HOW WOULD YOU RESPOND IF I SAID YOU WERE UNSUITABLE FOR THIS JOB?

A comparable question to 'What would you say if I said you had performed badly today?' and asked for the same reasons. Give another, appropriate answer. 'I'd be upset, as I'm convinced I'm the best person for the post. I've the qualifications for it – a Higher National Diploma in hospitality management. I've had the experience – three years in the same job at the Newbury Hotel. I've the right personality too – friendly but firm with staff, pleasant and patient with guests. I want the job as well, more than any I've ever come across. I am the right person for this job.' Spot-on – you have remained cool and rebutted the suggestion without causing offence, *and* have promoted your strengths once more.

HANDLING OFFBEAT QUESTIONS: AN ACTION CHECKLIST

Check out the following questions and write down the points you wish to make in reply to them.

Who is your favourite historical figure?

What do you think of me as an interviewer?

Who or what has been the biggest influence on your life?

What would you say if I said you had performed badly today?

What is the most embarrassing thing that has ever happened to you?

How would you respond if I said you were unsuitable for this job?

What would you most like to do with your life?

What do you think of the Government's handling of recent events?

What have you heard about this organisation?

WHAT DO YOU THINK OF THE GOVERNMENT'S HANDLING OF RECENT EVENTS?

Various questions may arise about the Government and other regulatory bodies, and could be quite specific – 'What is your opinion of the Government's attitude towards public sector pay claims?', 'How do you feel about our trade association's new code of practice?' and 'What is your view of the watchdog body's latest report on our industry?' are examples. These questions are all asked to see whether you have a broad grasp of what is going on around you, can talk about the subjects and – as important – share the same basic outlook as the organisation. Not surprisingly, your interviewer will prefer to recruit a person with similar rather than contrasting views.

Thus, your reply should be something like this: 'Well, it's a complex matter, of course. On the one hand, the Government states that it has to take this approach in order to combat inflation. The industry says that its approach will lead to widespread closures and redundancies. I can see that both sides have valid points and expect they will be proved equally correct, but as your chairman, Sir Anthony Reynolds, said, that's of little consolation to the unfortunate people who lost their employment.' This is a solid response – you are well prepared, able to see both arguments and can tell the interviewer what he or she wants to hear.

CHECKING KEY FACTS

Inevitably, a few facts will have been ignored during the topics covered earlier on in your conversation and may be dealt with together towards the end of the interview. These questions could arise at this stage:

– Why has this question been left unanswered?
– Do you have a clean driving licence?

- May I see your certificates?
- Are you willing to have a medical examination?
- What will your referees say about you?

WHY HAS THIS QUESTION BEEN LEFT UNANSWERED?
If you failed to answer a question or complete a section on the application form, the interviewer will probably spot and ask you about it, because he or she wants to know if it is simply an oversight or an attempt to gloss over a weakness. Typically, you might be several years older than the stated age range and resent this requirement because you know you can do the job well. Perhaps you were unemployed for a period of time and feel embarrassed about this – although it is far from uncommon and certainly not a stigma these days.

Having made an error, you could say something along the lines of: 'I'm sorry, I was concentrating so much on telling you about my attributes for the job that I must have overlooked it. Sorry about that. The answer to the question is . . .' A minor oversight is unlikely to count against you *unless* the form is short and the question or section should have been seen, or an eye for detail is essential for this position. In these cases, you are clearly in difficulty as you will appear either half-hearted about your application or incompetent, neither of which will further your cause.

If you deliberately omitted an answer because of your age, unemployment or whatever, you should explain your reasons and why you believe you are suitable for the job. For example: 'I didn't state my age because I'm five years above the required age range and felt I'd be rejected automatically if I put it on the form. I just had to apply for the job, though, as I'm so right for it in every other way. You can see that my education, qualifications, training and employment have given me the skills, knowledge and experience needed to do the job – and I want it so much that I had to come along.' Fingers crossed, and you will stay in contention.

DO YOU HAVE A CLEAN DRIVING LICENCE?

This is a straightforward question which is asked to check that
you meet this particular requirement. It needs no more than a
simple and substantiated answer – 'Yes, I do. I brought it with
me to show you . . . Ah, here it is . . .' Similar questions such as
'Do you have a telephone answering machine?', 'Do you have a
fax machine?', 'Do you have a reliable car?' and so on should
also be answered in a positive manner and supported with proof
whenever possible. As example: 'Yes, I've a fax machine – the
number is 0394 49362' and 'Yes, I've a three-year-old Sierra, it's
the red one down there in the car park.'

MAY I SEE YOUR CERTIFICATES?

Not surprisingly, the interviewer may want to actually see any
certificates and diplomas that you claim to have to make sure
you really do possess them and have obtained the stated grades.
Always take along the appropriate documents to the interview
so that you can give a clear and resounding response – 'Yes, of
course. Here they are . . .' This is much better than subsequently
sending in the originals which may go astray, posting photocopies that the interviewer could view with suspicion as these
are easy to forge, or delivering documents yourself since this
might make you seem pushy. Have them to hand to satisfy your
interviewer there and then.

ARE YOU WILLING TO HAVE A MEDICAL
EXAMINATION?

This question is raised increasingly often nowadays as organisations try to ensure that their new recruits are healthy by in-
sisting that they are examined by a company doctor or local
general practitioner before being taken on. Obviously, an
organisation does not want to employ someone who is likely to
be off sick as this will cost unnecessary time and money, to
cover absences, pay wages and so forth. To win a job offer, your
answer must be positive and backed up with a reassuring comment, if possible. Say something like this: 'Yes, I'd be more than

happy to have a medical for the job. I am very fit and healthy and didn't miss a day's work during my four years at Langstons. My boss, Mrs Pertwee, will confirm this.'

WHAT WILL YOUR REFEREES SAY ABOUT YOU?

A clever question, used to discover what your referees might say, *and* to hear how you talk about them, and their comments. It is wise to refer to the referees in a respectful manner, and to be modest about their statements – but do take the opportunity to mention your strengths too! For example, you could say: 'I hope that Mr Gibbs, my personal tutor, and Miss Singh, the course leader, will both confirm that I am punctual, attentive and hard-working. I've talked through my application with them, and they've said they think I'm well suited to the job.' Whatever you say, avoid sounding overfamiliar or bragging about how they will praise you. You may believe it will make you appear wonderful, but the interviewer will not.

CHECKING KEY FACTS: AN ACTION CHECKLIST

You need to consider these questions carefully, and prepare
loose and flexible answers.

Why has this question been left unanswered?

Do you have a clean driving licence?

May I see your certificates?

Are you willing to have a medical examination?

What will your referees say about you?

7 THE CLOSING STAGES

Dealing with the Final Questions
Leaving the Interview Room
Going Home

7 THE CLOSING STAGES

Having found out as much as possible about you by discussing your education, qualifications, training, employment, personality and other, miscellaneous topics, your interviewer will now draw the interview to a close. You need to know how to deal with his or her final questions and leave the interview room properly. Following on, you also have to learn what you should do when going home and thereafter, to try to ensure that you are a winner on this occasion.

DEALING WITH THE FINAL QUESTIONS

With all of the key questions asked, the interviewer probably wants to round off the interview as promptly as possible, and will attempt to do this by raising various questions to tidy matters up. You still have a number of points to put across though, so be ready with your answers to these questions:

– How much notice do you have to give?
– May I approach your referees?
– Do you have any questions?
– Is there anything else you wish to tell me?
– Can you find your own way out?

HOW MUCH NOTICE DO YOU HAVE TO GIVE?
This is a very positive question – and an extremely encouraging sign, as the interviewer would not be talking to you about handing in your notice unless an offer was being considered. He or

she wants to hear that you are so keen and enthusiastic about the job that you wish to start work as soon as possible. At the same time, your interviewer wants to see you adopt a fair and responsible attitude towards your existing employment. After all, if you indicate that you are prepared to walk out on your current job tomorrow, he or she will be concerned that you will do the same again in the future. No one will employ a person who might do this.

You could say something along these lines: 'Well, I'd like to start work here as soon as I can, but I've promised my boss, Mr Platek, that I'd give him one month's notice so he'll have time to find a replacement for me. I get on well with him, though, and I'm sure he'll let me leave as soon as he's sorted out some cover for my work.' If you are unemployed at the moment, the alternative 'If I offer the job to you, when could you start work?' makes your reply that much easier. To win the job you provide a short and definite response – 'Tomorrow morning, at nine o'clock!'

MAY I APPROACH YOUR REFEREES?

Another encouraging question! Before recruiting you, the interviewer will want to obtain references to substantiate or disprove your comments about yourself. He or she may prefer to contact some referees such as school teachers and former employees before making an offer, although a current employer who might be unaware that you are job hunting should not be approached until after an offer has been made, and permission has been granted by you. Thus, your interviewer now wants to be given the go-ahead to get in touch with your referees and may also be hoping to be invited to contact them by telephone rather than in writing, as off-the-record conversations will be more informative and revealing.

Your answer must be warm and welcoming: 'Yes, of course. I'd be more than happy for you to approach my last two employers, Ethel Wilson at Gayther's and Nick Harrison at Mercury. Let me give you their phone numbers so that you can call them – Mrs Wilson's is 0394 877051, and Mr Harrison's is 0903 271975.' Do not feel embarrassed about asking your interviewer not to approach your existing employer yet. This is neither an unexpected nor an unreasonable request, and the interviewer should not be disturbed by an additional comment such as this: 'As I haven't yet discussed this job application with my current boss, Mr Aziz, I'd prefer it if you didn't contact him at this stage.'

DO YOU HAVE ANY QUESTIONS?

Here, the interviewer is trying to find out whether you really do want the job. If you do, he or she will expect you to ask questions about the organisation and the job, to fill in any gaps in your knowledge. Remember that you are still attempting to win this job, so raise questions which will show you in a good light and promote your strengths. As examples, you might say: 'Yes, I'm keen to keep learning, and wonder if you can tell me about your training scheme' or 'Yes, I'm very hard-working and want to know what my targets would be in this post.'

With this question, it is as important to know what *not* to say. 'No, I've no questions' makes you sound disinterested and even anxious to go home as soon as possible – so avoid stating anything like this. Questions seeking information which should have been easy to obtain through simple research ought to be avoided too. Asking about your new boss, tasks and duties, colleagues, the type of person required for the job and so on is unwise – you should know all of these topics inside out *and* have proved it by commenting on them at appropriate moments earlier on in the interview. If you have not, you will seem half-hearted about the position.

Similarly, steer away from questions about the salary, fringe benefits, holidays and the like. These suggest a self-centred attitude to your work which will not appeal to the interviewer, who is hoping for a more generous, fair-minded approach. Do not put your interviewer on the spot by asking him or her to evaluate your performance, comment on your suitability, tell you when the decision will be made or even if you have got the job. All of these requests will simply embarrass and alienate the interviewer and make you appear to be an insensitive and unrealistic fool. Never raise trivial questions either – 'Where is the 76 bus stop?' or 'Which is the quickest way to the tube from here?' will show you in a poor light.

IS THERE ANYTHING ELSE YOU WISH TO TELL ME?

This is probably one of the most popular questions asked to round off the interview, and to give you a final opportunity to win that job. Your interviewer expects you to summarise your attributes for the post, and to tell him or her how much you want it – so do this! 'Yes, I believe I'm the best person for the job. I have all of the qualifications that you require – and I've had the experience too. I have the right personality for the work – I'm friendly, hard-working and ambitious. I've always wanted to do this job for as long as I can remember, and everything I've done – education, qualifications, training and employment – has been with the aim of getting the job. That's why I'm here now.'

CAN YOU FIND YOUR OWN WAY OUT?

At last – the final question! This is asked for one reason only, and that is to provide you with an absolutely clear and unmistakable signal that the interview is over. Say this in reply: 'Yes, thank you for seeing me today, Mrs Kimble, I hope you're convinced that I'm the right person for this job and I look forward to hearing from you soon.' Hopefully, your interviewer will then tell you when to expect a decision, probably within the next few days. Do not be disheartened that the interview has not concluded with a job offer – that will come later when *all* of the interviews have taken place and your interviewer can reach a balanced decision. That is only fair to the other interviewees.

DEALING WITH THE FINAL QUESTIONS: AN ACTION CHECKLIST

Mull over these questions, and jot down notes so that you are better prepared to answer them.

How much notice do you have to give?

May I approach your referees?

Do you have any questions?

Is there anything else you wish to tell me?

Can you find your own way out?

LEAVING THE INTERVIEW ROOM

As your interviewer asks the last question, or immediately after your answer, he or she will probably stand up, smile and hold out a hand. Follow the interviewer's lead, whatever it may be – getting to your feet, smiling and shaking hands, as appropriate. If more than one person interviewed you, look at each in turn, thanking them and shaking their hands, as relevant. 'Thank you, Mr Devries . . . Mrs Marks . . . thank you, Mr Hume', and so forth. Make sure that you address them by the correct names, and pronounce these properly. If in doubt, simply smile warmly and thank them.

Most likely, you will then be shown to the door by the interviewer, but not guided back to the reception area as this should be easy for you to find, second time around. Also, he or she may want to make notes about you whilst the thoughts are still fresh, could wish to discuss you with colleagues, or whatever. Do not ask for directions, even if it means you will spend ten minutes looking for the exit. To ask makes you appear incompetent and helpless, and could irritate the interviewer if he or she has to show you the way. Go to the door, turn, thank him or her again and say goodbye – then get lost!

If the interview room is on the sixth floor or tucked away in a maze of corridors, your interviewer may take you to reception. Be prepared to walk along in companionable silence if there is nothing left to say, or make small talk again, as appropriate. If the interviewer decides to mention the weather or your journey home, respond in a friendly manner, just speaking enough to nudge that conversation on. Keep it moving by referring to the size of the lift, the decor or whatever catches your attention. Do your best to minimise the awkwardness of these few minutes through idle chitchat. Arriving at reception, smile, thank your interviewer for showing you out, and say goodbye.

As the interviewer disappears back into the lift or up the stairs, go and pick up your overcoat and baggage – it is surprising how many interviewees leave these behind and have to return later, much to their embarrassment. Then ask the receptionist to give you the initials and correct spelling of your interviewer's name, if you do not already possess these details. You need them for a follow-up letter, which might just provide you with that edge in the selection process. Thank the receptionist for his or her time, and for being so helpful. You can now breathe a sigh of relief as you leave the building. It is all over – almost!

GOING HOME

On the way home, review your performance at the interview. Were you as well prepared as you might have been? Did you arrive on time? Were you tidy and clean? Did you relax and stay calm, without being impatient or argumentative? You must think carefully about these various do's and don'ts of interviewing success. Did you look at and listen to the interviewer, and avoid becoming overfamiliar? Did you speak clearly, without talking too much, being irrelevant, criticising others or showing off? In short, were you the winning interviewee?

Mull over what you learned at the interview. Did you discover anything new about the organisation? Perhaps you were impressed by the modern business equipment, or put off by the rude and sullen staff. Did you find out more about the job? Possibly, you were pleased to hear about the excellent training scheme available for new recruits, or disheartened to be told about the unrealistic targets you would be expected to achieve. Did you learn anything else about the type of person needed for the job? Perhaps the interviewer probed you about requirements which you had not uncovered, and can or cannot fulfil. You may decide that your personality, strengths and weaknesses are more, or less, suited to the post than you originally believed.

Think about what you have learned about interviews from this occasion. What was the interview itself like? Perhaps this was your first panel interview or the only time that you have been interviewed in a noisy office, or for such a long period.

How did you feel about your interviewer? He or she may have been experienced or inexperienced, leading the conversation on or allowing you to control it. What were the questions like? You could have been asked many open questions which were easy to answer, or had to work extra hard to overcome a succession of closed and limited ones. Whatever happens, this will have been an excellent learning process for you.

At home, type or carefully write a letter to the interviewer, briefly thanking him or her for seeing you, summarising your qualities and restating your interest in the job. Post it off with a first-class stamp that same day, or the following one if this is not possible. Hopefully, this polite letter will set you apart from the other interviewees, remind your interviewer of your strengths, and tip the balance in your favour. Then carry on with your job hunting, waiting to hear from the interviewer – sending more letters or telephoning him or her for a progress report or a decision will irritate and annoy, and might lose you the job.

Within a week or so, you will receive a telephone call or (more likely) a letter from your interviewer. If you are rejected – as all but one of the many applicants will be – take time out to review your performance again, think about the organisation, job and the person required and contemplate your personality, strengths and weaknesses once more, to work out why you were not offered the job. Learn from this experience, and gain from it. If you are friendly and reasonable, telephone or write to the interviewer asking him or her to indicate why you were turned down. He or she may tell you, which will be helpful to you on future occasions, but do not become angry or unpleasant if the interviewer prefers not to discuss matters. After all, there were probably hundreds of applicants, and not everyone can expect a blow-by-blow assessment.

Hopefully, you will receive a job offer, perhaps subject only to satisfactory references and a medical examination, which should not cause problems for you. Decide whether you wish to accept this offer, bearing in mind that the interview may have revealed information about the organisation and job which you were previously unaware of. Should you decide to decline, reject the offer in a polite and pleasant manner, explaining your reasons if these will not give offence. Always remember that you may wish to join the organisation in another capacity in the future, or could cross paths with the interviewer again elsewhere, so you must avoid upsetting anyone now.

More likely, you will wish to accept the job offer, albeit subject to negotiation. Knowing that you are the winner from so many applicants puts you in a good position, so you can push for a better salary, improved fringe benefits, holidays and so on. Telephone or write to take up the offer and discuss terms and conditions with your interviewer. Get the best deal that you can, because you deserve it. You did your research, knew you were the right person, tackled the interview properly, answered those one hundred and one questions – and got the job!

GOING HOME: AN ACTION CHECKLIST

Your interview will have been an excellent learning opportunity for you. Note down what you learned about the following:

The Do's of Interviewing Success

The Ideal Employee

The Don'ts of Interviewing Success

The Interview

The Organisation

The Interviewer

The Job

The Questions

101 QUESTIONS: A CHECKLIST

FURTHER READING

Answer the Question: Get the Job! is probably one of several books that you will study during your careers/job hunting/interviews/ employment reading. Here is a short list of other, recommended texts on these subjects which are worth obtaining from your local bookshop or library. If you cannot find them there, contact the appropriate publisher for assistance.

An A-Z of Careers and Jobs by Diane Burston, £9.99, paperback. Published by Kogan Page Limited, 120 Pentonville Road, London N1 9JN. Telephone: 071 278 0433.

Detailing over 350 careers and jobs, this book is a useful starting point for all school and college leavers who are thinking about the future. It is full of up-to-date information on employment issues.

How to Choose a Career by Vivien Donald, £6.99, paperback. Published by Kogan Page Limited, 120 Pentonville Road, London N1 9JN. Telephone: 071 278 0433.

A first-rate guide for young people making career choices, this text offers advice and guidance on traditional career paths plus opportunities in growth areas such as leisure, entertainment and financial services.

The Kogan Page Guides to Careers, £5.99, paperback. Published by Kogan Page Limited, 120 Pentonville Road, London, N1 9JN. Telephone: 071 278 0433.

Aimed at school and college leavers, this series of practical guides details jobs across a wide range of employment fields. Whether you are considering a career in alternative medicine or social work, shops and stores or the travel industry, the series probably incorporates a title of relevance to you.

How to Win at Job Hunting by Iain Maitland, £6.99, paperback. Published by Century Business, Random House, 20 Vauxhall Bridge Road, London SW1V 2SA. Telephone: 071 973 9000.

A clear, step-by-step introduction to finding the right job, written mainly for younger job seekers. It will give you that all-important edge needed for job hunting success.

How to Get a Job Abroad by Roger Jones, £9.99, paperback. Published by How To Books Limited, Plymbridge House, Estover Road, Plymouth, Devon PL6 7PZ. Telephone: 0752 695745.

One of several titles about job hunting overseas published by How To Books, this is a concise and understandable guide to a potentially complex subject. Other, equally interesting, titles include *How to Get a Job in America, How to Get a Job in Australia* and *How to Get a Job in Europe*.

Talk Small! by Pete Daly, £5.99, paperback. Published by Kogan Page Limited, 120 Pentonville Road, London N1 9JN. Telephone: 071 278 0433.

This is a humorous and extremely readable book about making small talk in a variety of situations, with helpful advice on body language too. Check it out – this will enable you to learn how to chat effectively on the way to the interview room, and during the early stages of your interview.

Further reading

How to Win at Interviews by Iain Maitland, £5.99, paperback. Published by Century Business, Random House, 20 Vauxhall Bridge Road, London SW1V 2SA. Telephone: 071 973 9000.

Succinct and clearly written, this is an introductory text about selection interviews, with information and suggestions about how to be a successful interviewee and win that job! Employment interviews are detailed too and appropriate guidance is given.

How to Negotiate Your Salary by Alan Jones, £7.99, paperback. Published by Century Business, Random House, 20 Vauxhall Bridge Road, London SW1V 2SA. Telephone: 071 973 9000.

Whether you have to negotiate your salary for an existing or a new job, this practical guide tells you all you need to know to obtain the package you want. It is worth a cover-to-cover read, to boost your chances of success.

How to Know Your Rights at Work by Robert Spicer, £6.99, paperback. Published by How To Books Limited, Plymbridge House, Estover Road, Plymouth, Devon PL6 ZPZ. Telephone: 0752 695745.

This book looks at your employment rights and responsibilities. Accessible and easy to absorb, it is essential reading for all would-be *and* long-serving employees.

The Barclays Guide to Managing Staff for the Small Business by Iain Maitland, £9.99, paperback. Published by Blackwell Business, 108 Cowley Road, Oxford OX4 1JF. Telephone: 0865 791100.

This is a quick, all-round introduction to a host of employment topics of relevance to employers *and* employees. Induction, disciplinary, grievance, counselling and exit interviews are covered in a concise and straightforward manner.

The Mid-Career Action Guide by Derek and Fred Kemp, £8.99, paperback. Published by Kogan Page Limited, 120 Pentonville Road, London N1 9JN. Telephone: 071 278 0433.

If you are planning to move jobs in the near future, this hands-on guide is for you. It encourages readers to review their skills and attributes prior to making a move, and uses appropriate case histories to illustrate key points.

Making a Comeback by Margaret Korving, £5.99, paperback. Published by Century Business, Random House, 20 Vauxhall Bridge Road, London SW1V 2SA. Telephone: 071 973 9000.

This is a useful book of interest to all women returning to work after a career break. It is full of helpful information about the do's and don'ts of making a successful comeback into the employment marketplace.

USEFUL ADDRESSES

Your careers/job hunting/interviews/employment research may benefit from contacting various relevant organisations and talking to their staff. In addition to job centres, recruitment agencies and libraries, here are some other, helpful contacts which you might not have thought of:

Advisory, Conciliation and Arbitration Services (ACAS),
11–12 St James Square, London SW1Y 4LA.
Telephone: 071 210 3000.

ACAS provides good, solid advice on all employment issues from induction through to counselling and dismissal, including interviews. Various regional offices are dotted around the United Kingdom.

Central Office of the Industrial Tribunals,
93 Ebury Bridge Road, London SW1W 8RE.
Telephone: 071 730 9161.

This is the organisation to approach if you believe you have been discriminated against during the selection process, or thereafter. Get in touch if you were upset by those questions which invaded your privacy – the organisation will tell you about your rights. There are other, regional offices across the country.

Commission for Racial Equality,
10–12 Allington Street, London SW1E 5EH.
Telephone: 071 828 7022.

The CRE can help you if you feel you have been discriminated against on racial grounds whether during recruitment or at work. This is *the* organisation to contact in these circumstances.

The Department of Employment,
Caxton House, Tothill Street, London SW1H 9NF.
Telephone: 071 272 3000.

A valuable source of information on all employment-related matters. The Department can assist you in many ways, not least with regard to all types of interviews.

Equal Opportunities Commission,
Overseas House, Quay Street, Manchester M3 3HN.
Telephone: 061 833 9244.

If you believe you have had a raw deal because of your sex, age or race, talk to the Commission's staff, for hands-on advice and guidance which is appropriate to your specific situation.

Race Relations Employment Advisory Service,
11 Belgrave Road, London SW1V 1RB.
Telephone: 071 834 6644.

As the name suggests, information and advice is available on race relations. A helpful organisation which is worth contacting if such matters are of particular significance to you.

INDEX

Referring to the Contents pages and 101 Questions: A Checklist on pages 153–6 should enable you to discover the information that you want, perhaps second time around. Alternatively, this concise index will point you in the right direction. It concentrates on broad headings and references rather than minutiae as it is unlikely that you will wish to be reminded that 'snoring' was mentioned once on page 105, or will want to check out thirty seven passing references to 'appearance' before finding that the key details you need to know about are on pages 24 and 34.